Taking the *anxiety* out of taking **Tests**

Taking the *anxiety* out of taking **Tests**

A Step-By-Step Guide

Susan Johnson

BARNES
&NOBLE
B O O K S
NEW YORK

Publisher's Note

This publication is designed to provide accurate and authoritative information in regard to the subject matter covered. It is sold with the understanding that the publisher is not engaged in rendering psychological, financial, legal, or other professional services. If expert assistance or counseling is needed, the services of a competent professional should be sought.

To My Sweetie

Contents

Introduction

Test-taking anxiety is the feeling of fear you have when your performance is about to be evaluated. When you experience this type of anxiety,
your abilities to think and to pay attention plummet, right at a time
when you need them most.

As you might expect, this sense of overwhelming fear makes performing the task you're being tested on much more difficult than it
would be if your thoughts were clear and your attention was focused.
In fact, research has shown that there is a *negative correlation* between
the levels of anxiety that students have and their test scores. In other
words, the more anxious you become, the lower your test score will
probably be.

Whenever you feel extremely anxious, you will usually entertain
a series of distorted thoughts. You think, "What's wrong with me?" or
"Why am I so stupid?" or "I'll never be able to do this!" and you
respond to these negative thoughts by becoming even more afraid.
Each time you take a test, you have the same thoughts, and these
thoughts (and your emotional reactions to them) take up a certain
amount of your attention during the test. Splitting your attention in
this way limits the amount of information that you can process and
inhibits your ability to figure out exactly what you're being asked to
do. Consequently, you answer the questions more slowly than you
would if you weren't anxious, and you may frequently answer with
the wrong information.

Anxiety also hurts your self-confidence—and low self-confidence
can contribute to low test scores. Psychologists have found that people
who have high levels of test-taking anxiety tend to present negative

descriptions of themselves on personality questionnaires. During tests, these students often feel helpless and unable to influence the outcome, and they tend to give up quickly whenever an obstacle to answering a question arises. In turn, each experience of not doing well on a test contributes to a still more negative self-image. Studies indicate that this lack of self-confidence often carries over from the testing room into other situations and can inhibit the way an individual reacts to different experiences.

Therapies That Help

Although many people consistently get lower grades because they suffer from test-taking anxiety, they often avoid this problem until they reach a point when they feel incapable of actually entering a test room. This is extremely unfortunate, since test-taking anxiety responds well to specific therapeutic interventions. Over the past several decades, numerous studies have determined exactly which methods will best help those who suffer from this debilitating condition. Two observations were made:

First, cognitive-behavioral therapies have proved to be the most effective way of treating test-taking anxiety. These include:

- Relaxation techniques

- Irrational-thought monitoring

- Systematic Desensitization therapy

- Behavior Visualization therapy

Second, study skills training can help students reorganize study material so that less of their attention is needed to store and recall information in their memory. This means that, even though their attention may be split between the test they are taking and their internal reactions, good study skills training will help these students cover more of the material on the test with the attention they have available.

The conclusion reached by most researchers is that a strategy combining cognitive and behavioral therapy with study skills training is the most powerful method of lowering test-taking anxiety and enhancing academic performance.

Anxiety versus Fear

Psychologists often assign different definitions to the terms "anxiety" and "fear." They define fear as the apprehension that a specific thing will or won't happen. You could, for example, fear that you will fail a test, or that someone will reject you, or that you won't achieve a specific goal. Anxiety, on the other hand, is often used to connote a feeling that is much more vague. You might feel anxious that you're not good enough, or that you will lose control, or that something awful is about to happen. These differences are largely subjective, and you may find it difficult to tell whether you're afraid of doing poorly on an upcoming test or anxious about your ability to do well. Yet both of these emotions elicit exactly the same physical response, which includes rapid heart rate, quick, shallow breathing, sweating palms, increased muscular tension, and elevated blood pressure. Since the differences between fear and anxiety are hazy, and the physical reactions are exactly the same, these words will be used interchangeably throughout this text.

This Book Is Different

This book gathers the most effective techniques used for lowering test-taking anxiety into one volume. Each chapter describes a specific skill or group of skills and provides examples and exercises that will show you how you can think and behave differently in the academic arena. Throughout the text, suggestions are given on how to focus your concentration when your mind wanders from the exercise you are practicing or the material you are studying.

How to Use This Book

The best way to reduce your level of test-taking anxiety is to use a mixture of cognitive and behavioral techniques combined with good study skills, here is the most effective way to use this book:

Read and practice the exercises in chapters 1, 2, and 3 first. Together these chapters explain the basic information and skills you will need to understand your anxiety and keep it from affecting your test performance.

Chapter 1 gives you an overview of fear: why you are afraid, how fear affects you mentally and physically, and what you need to do to move through your fear. It then explains how your attention works and details those things you can do to strengthen your ability to concentrate on one thing at a time. Chapters 2 and 3 explain basic methods for calming down your body and your mind when you become afraid. Chapter 2 covers numerous techniques that will allow you to physically relax, even when you are in a threatening situation. Chapter 3 explains how your thoughts work when you are afraid and how you can keep them from escalating your sense of fear.

Next read chapters 4 and 5, which detail the two cognitive techniques that will help you alleviate the stress that test taking causes.

Chapter 4 explains *Systematic Desensitization,* a method of exposing yourself to the thing you fear in small, measured doses. Chapter 5 describes *Behavior Visualization* (also known as Covert Modeling), a technique that guides you through a fear-producing scene in your imagination. This mental rehearsing allows you to approach each test with a greater sense of confidence. Many have found using either one of these techniques a valuable way to decrease their anxiety in the test room. Try both and then choose the one that works best for you.

Finally, read chapters 6 and 7. These are the chapters that will introduce you to effective study skills. Chapter 6 describes the process of procrastination and shows how you can more effectively manage your time. Chapter 7 describes how your brain learns, how you can learn material quickly, and how to remember it at the critical moment. You are the best judge of which specific skills will help you prepare for a test. Pick the skills that seem appropriate and use them when you study.

To make this book work for you, you need to be an active reader. Do all the exercises. Write out the ones that need to be written and practice the relaxation and awareness exercises often. Trying to use these skills without practicing them first is like trying to lift two hundred pounds without first developing your muscles. The more you practice these exercises, the more successful your test-taking experiences will become. And the more successful test-taking experiences you have, the less anxiety you will feel.

If you feel apprehensive about actually doing this work, you haven't yet made a true commitment to change the way you react to being evaluated. You may want to sit down and review how your anxiety is blocking you from the things you want to do and decide whether these things are truly important to you.

Remember that any time you face a task that seems difficult or painful in some way, it always becomes a bit easier if you talk to someone about it. Please, discuss your anxiety and the work you are doing with this book with other people. You may be surprised at the range of help that others are able to offer. Other students may be able to tell you how they fight off their own anxiety or suggest tricks they use to do well on a test. Parents, counselors, and friends can offer understanding, commiseration, useful information, and bits of wisdom that may help to keep you motivated. So, talk to as many people as you comfortably can about your test-taking anxiety and how you are working to cope with it. You'll find it'll make the long road a little less bumpy.

I

About Working with Fear

A Word about Fear

As our world becomes more competitive and dangerous, and less personal and secure, more and more of us are responding to the stress in our environment with fear. We feel as though we have no control over our lives, and we fear what will happen as a result. Although this has always been the case, today's fast-paced world makes the circumstances of our lives seem a little more precariously perched. Many of us often fear that something unexpected could happen that would make our lives seemingly intolerable: losing a loved one, losing a job, coping with our own failing health, or being the victim of a crime. At any moment, our lives could take a nasty turn and change in a way that may seem unbearable.

And, of course, this is all true. These are all possibilities. In a way, we are right to fear these things, at least some of the time. This fear tells us that we need to take whatever measures we can to avert these disasters. But often our fear expands beyond its usefulness. Instead of being an alarm that goes off when something dangerous might happen, it malfunctions and sounds much too often and at the wrong times. Once this happens, our fears have no meaning. Instead of being a useful means of detecting danger, they have become an emotional habit that prevents us from functioning in the ways our lives demand.

To better understand how fear operates, you need to understand the physiological changes that take place in your body when you're afraid. Your nervous system is wired to react to everything you perceive as dangerous as though it were a physical threat. It is preparing you to deal with this threat by either running from it or fighting it. As soon as your brain believes that a threat is present, your nervous system will start to produce more stress hormones than it normally does. These additional hormones, the most well known of which is adrenaline, will change your body in the following ways:

- Your heart will pump about four times the volume of blood that it normally would, sending more blood to your larger muscles.

- Your breath rate will increase, causing more oxygen to be drawn into your lungs; this extra oxygen will then be sent to your larger muscles.

- The sweat glands that regulate your body temperature will become activated, which will protect your body from becoming overheated.

- Your thinking process will shut down momentarily while your concentration becomes focused on how you need to act to avoid or vanquish the threat.

- Your pupils increase in size, expanding your field of vision.

- Your blood coagulates faster to prevent hemorrhaging.

- Your digestive system shuts down, and the blood that usually flows here is rerouted to your muscles. You may experience this blood rerouting as "butterflies in the stomach."

In the early part of this century, the physiologist Walter B. Cannon studied this phenomenon in animals and called it the *fight-or-flight response*. It is the only way your body knows how to respond when you're afraid, no matter what it is that you're afraid of. This hyper-alert state can be a very valuable reaction when there is an actual physical threat. However, more often than not, this isn't the case. In this day and age, most people's fears tend to be based on things that might cause them emotional pain, not physical harm: Will that person like me? Will I be laid off next month? Will my children be healthy? Will I achieve my goals? Commonly these fears are directed at the future: the potential rejection, the imagined foreclosure, the dreaded disease, the test that looms on the horizon. If you were truly afraid of any one of these situations, even though they're not a tangible threat to your physical well-being, you would experience the fight-or-flight response. However, the option of fighting or fleeing is often impossible, or at best inappropriate.

Once you understand this, the way you react when you're about to take a test may make more sense to you. When you feel afraid, your body has geared up to fight off or run from whatever bad thing seems to be threatening you. This is *not* an appropriate response to taking a test, or to most of the other things that you, and almost everyone else, find frightening. So there you are, stuck with all of these physiological changes that make you want to run away or hit someone just at the time when you need to sit down and take your midterm. This state of hyper-alertness is not conducive to remembering facts and figuring out problems. Your thoughts will be screaming that this test is the worst thing in the world and that there is no way you can possibly do it. Your body will refuse to sleep, and your muscles will store a lot of tension. You may feel so threatened at the prospect of taking a test that the last thing you'll want to do is enter the test room. Your body is reacting as though entering this room will put you face-to-face with a dragon.

Unfortunately, simply understanding how fear works won't necessarily make it any easier to control. Telling yourself that there is really nothing here that can harm you isn't enough to calm your nerves. The work you'll need to do is of an inner nature and involves both your mind and your body. You can begin changing your response to fear by learning how to release the tension in your body as best you can and watching your thoughts as they come and go while resisting the temptation to get caught up in their story line.

However, staying in the situation that makes you afraid and doing what you need to do can almost seem like a suicidal act. Your nervous system has amped up the energy in your body because you believe that something is about to "get" you. It seems plain crazy to resist reacting to this extraordinary physical energy and to resist listening to the thoughts that are telling you how dangerous everything is and to just stay in the situation that is making you afraid. It feels as though the imagined danger could rise up and clobber you at any time. This is the reason that many people prefer to live a limited life rather than learn how to get beyond reacting to the situations that scare them. To them, it feels much too scary to drop their defenses in the presence of something frightening. Staying in an alarmed state, even if that means feeling anxious most of the time, seems much safer than letting down their guard. Most anxious people prefer to stay anxious because anxiety feels safe.

Transforming Fear

Whenever you encounter test taking, whether you're physically walking into the test room or simply thinking about picking up a book to study, you may respond automatically and unconsciously with a fearful reaction. Your goal, as you read this book and practice these exercises, is not to become unafraid. You may always feel fearful in certain situations. And there is nothing wrong with feeling afraid. Everyone feels fear to some degree. Fear only becomes a problem when it stops you from doing the things you want to do.

This book teaches you how to turn your fear level down to a point where you can function adequately, even though you're still afraid. By learning to focus your attention on what your body is feeling and what your mind is thinking as you react to a threatening situation, you'll be transforming your fear from an unconscious to a conscious activity. When you're aware of your fear, you can make choices about how you want to behave, instead of automatically reacting in ways that will help you escape from feeling your fear.

In the face of fear, whether that fear is large or small, your automatic response will often be to find a way to make yourself more comfortable. Usually you do this in one of two ways. You can find a diversion to pull your mind and attention somewhere else—for example, using drugs or alcohol, overeating, overworking, watching TV, compulsive shopping, and so on. Or you can find a way to avoid the threatening situation altogether—for example, becoming ill, procrastinating, or deciding that you really didn't want to do this threatening thing anyway. No matter which of these tactics you take, the end result is that you've created an escape hatch through which you can momentarily avoid the discomfort you would experience if you allowed yourself to be present for your fear.

Any time you give in to your fearful thoughts and sensations and in some way avoid truly experiencing them, you're making your fear more real. For instance, if one time you escape the fear of taking a test by getting a little "illness," then your fear of taking tests will become a little more solid. It felt good to avoid your fear this once. So good, in fact, that you find yourself wondering if the solution to your fear is to avoid your other tests. Maybe you could. Maybe you really don't need to go to school at all. Maybe you could just avoid everything that makes you afraid.

Thoughts like these are probably not unfamiliar to you. Sometimes you may believe them, and sometimes you won't. However, when you give in to these types of thoughts and actually do what they are telling you to, you're choosing avoidance over feeling your fear. This reinforces the idea that if you're going to feel better, you need to do something to actually change your feelings, an idea that just plain isn't true.

Awareness Is the Key

Most of the time, we focus our attention on things other than our thoughts and feelings. Our emotions may seem so uncomfortable or overwhelming that we can't muster the attention it takes to actually experience them. Instead, we occupy the major part of our attention with other things—the ball game, last night's date, tomorrow's test, the work fiasco, our best friend's love life—while many of the fearful thoughts and inner sensations continue just beyond the edge of consciousness. Consequently, we're often so busy worrying about things that we never truly experience much of the life we are living, right here and right now.

The key to working through test-taking anxiety, or through any anxiety, is to develop awareness of your thoughts and physical sensations moment by moment. When you experience fear with awareness, you'll be creating a situation in which you can choose what you want to do and how you want to act, instead of reacting in the same old automatic ways. The more often you have this experience of being able to choose your reactions, the more control you will have over how you live your life. And, once you perceive that you do have control, you'll be able to let yourself become more and more relaxed. So, whether a sensation feels bad or good, or whether you like a thought or not, you need to learn to pull your attention into your body and just stay with your thoughts and sensations, whatever they may be.

Over time, as you practice pulling your attention away from your compelling thoughts and putting your awareness on your fearful thoughts and sensations, you'll find that you can enter the threatening scene, or entertain the threatening thought, and then just watch as your body and mind react. This repetitive refocusing of your awareness exercises the part of your mind that watches, or witnesses. In a way, it will seem almost as though there are two "you"s. There is the "you" who is thinking how awful this test is going to be and who feels afraid to take it, and there is the *you* who is watching the first "you" think this thought. If *you* are watching "you" have a thought, then you must be more than the fearful thought, and more than someone who has fearful thoughts. After all, if you are the person feeling afraid, who is this you who is watching? When you clearly understand that you are more than your thoughts, you'll realize that you don't need to behave in the ways that your thoughts demand.

By maintaining awareness of your fearful thoughts and sensations in this way, you'll eventually develop an emotional equilibrium that up until now you may have found elusive. You'll be able to catch your fearful thoughts more quickly, before you've had time to put a lot of emotional energy into creating and believing them, and return your attention to a more neutral point of focus (the sensations in your body, the material you're studying, the details of the room). When you repeatedly practice removing your attention from the fearful thought, you interrupt the build-up of your fear reaction. Your overall emotional disturbance will be less intense than it otherwise would be, and the time it takes you to emotionally "recover" will decrease.

How to Practice the Exercises with Awareness

You will be developing your awareness as you practice the exercises in this book. When you begin each exercise, your center of attention will be focused on what you need to accomplish in order to do that exercise. However, not many people can keep their mind steady on one thing for very long. In a short time, no matter how hard you try, your attention will move off the exercise and on to something else. As you work with each exercise, you'll need to practice being aware of the comings and goings of your point of focus as it flows from thought to thought, from physical sensation to physical sensation. Here are some suggestions for practicing awareness:

Label your thoughts. As soon as you notice your attention has drifted away from the exercise, label the thought that it drifted to. For example, tell yourself that you're having a thought about baseball, planning your speech, hearing the doorbell, feeling a pain in your toe. . . . Labeling your thoughts will help distance you from your thinking, so that instead of getting all wound up in the stories your thoughts are weaving, you'll be able to stand back and just observe them as they glide by. As soon as you've labeled your thought, return your attention to the exercise.

Pay attention to your physical sensations. Check in regularly to see how your body feels. Put your attention on the sensations in your body when you start each exercise, and then make a note of how any physical sensations change. For example, tell yourself that you're feeling the muscles in your abdomen let go, feeling your chest tighten, feeling the pins and needles in your leg. As soon as you notice your physical sensations, gently return your attention to the exercise.

Return your attention to your breath. Whenever you get lost— either you forget what you're doing, you don't remember the next step in the exercise, or you just space out for a while—return your attention to the rising and falling of your belly as you breathe. Just be with the sensation of breathing until the next step comes to you.

What Working with Awareness Teaches

When you practice the exercises in this book with awareness, you're not only learning the skill each exercise is designed to teach, but you'll also be learning that:

1. **You don't have to react to your thoughts.** Usually, your body is hooked up tightly to your thoughts. When you have one thought, quite often your body will jump up and respond to it. When you think that you want something, your body gets up to get it. When you think that you want to get rid of something, your body takes care of that too. Your life is a constant stream of thinking and then reacting to the content of your thoughts. Practicing awareness teaches you how to have a thought and just watch it, without doing anything about it. You'll see that when you have anxious thoughts about taking a test, and you feel like you have to *do something* to get rid of your fear, you really don't. Instead of acting on your thoughts, you'll notice them, accept them, and watch them vanish as others take their place.

2. **All of your thoughts and feelings, no matter how pressing they seem, will come and go.** You don't feel anxious all the time. Even during times when you think of yourself as "feeling anxious," there will be spaces within the anxiety in which you'll have thoughts of something else. Your thoughts are temporary, and your ability to watch them ultimately means that you are *more* than everything you think. Therefore, you don't need to believe in or be driven by your thoughts.

3. **You can be comfortable in your own body even when experiencing sensations of fear, anxiety, anger, or any other unpleasant emotion.** When you stay with your sensations from moment to moment, you'll realize that each sensation isn't inherently good or bad. It's the thoughts you have about your sensations that turn them into something more terrible or wonderful than they actually are. Instead of believing that you must get rid of unpleasant feelings, you can allow yourself to sink down into how each of these sensations actually feels. From this vantage point you'll be able to watch your emotions as they rise and fall. Eventually, you'll be able to reach a sense of calmness that is resting just beneath the agitation of your emotions.

4. **Each of your thoughts, as it rises up and then disappears, brings with it a certain emotional intensity.** Some thoughts are strongly pessimistic and bring with them feelings of anxiety, anger, and depression. Others are more positive and foster contentment and joy. And, still others are completely neutral. Thoughts that are intensely emotional—either intensely good or intensely awful—often recur over and over. You can become suddenly wrapped up in the story line and find it difficult to move your attention onto something else. Once you realize that the nature of thoughts is to come and go, you'll find it easier to resist becoming ensnared by the story they weave or the emotion they elicit. Instead of seeing your thoughts as "truth," you'll be able to regard them as "just more thinking."

5. Most of your thoughts focus on one of two categories: what things will make you feel better—how you can get them, and how you can keep them; and what things make you feel "bad" and how you can avoid them, or get rid of them.

In essence, everyone spends a lot of time wanting to feel better. This way of thinking is the root of the anxiety you feel. As soon as you think of something you want, you become afraid that you won't get it. As soon as you get it, you become afraid that you'll lose it. Or, once you get it, you become afraid that it really won't fix you up the way you thought it would, and then you'll have to get rid of it and find something else. We are all so sure that our happiness depends on whether or not we are getting what we want—good grades, the approval of others, nice things, a good job—that we don't realize we're really okay, right now, just as we are. It's this pattern of thinking that tosses your emotions around.

6. Fears are, more often than not, based on what you imagine will happen not what will actually happen. When you opt to do an exercise with awareness, regardless of what you're feeling, you'll discover that what actually happens will be entirely different from the way you imagined it. In real life, your actual test-taking experience will not only bear little resemblance to the way you thought it would be, but it'll be much less terrible than you imagined. It's almost as though the simple act of imagining an outcome will practically guarantee that something entirely different will happen. The fear reaction that it takes you so much energy to create, maintain, and avoid, is usually a useless protection against something that doesn't exist.

A Word about Attitude

It is helpful to approach the exercises in this book with a certain frame of mind. First, you need to begin each exercise realizing that practicing it is a valuable way to spend your time, and that rushing through the exercise will be counterproductive. Try to put aside everything that is bothering you, or pulling at you, for the amount of time you need to complete whatever exercise you are working on. If necessary, you can promise to give yourself plenty of time to worry about things later.

Second, as you practice these techniques, you'll have an almost constant stream of thoughts that is describing your experience to you and evaluating how you're doing. Don't take these thoughts seriously. Try not to worry about things like whether you're relaxing all of the muscle groups, or whether you're relaxing your muscles deeply enough, or whether you're relaxing your muscles at all. Simply follow the instructions to the best of your ability and understanding, then assume that you're doing everything right—your visualizations are vivid enough, your breathing is deep enough, your muscles are relaxed enough. When you find yourself thinking about how you're doing, just notice that you're having a judging thought, let the story line go, then return your attention to the exercise you were working on. The point of working with these exercises isn't to do them perfectly; it's to do the exercises as well as you can while being patient with and understanding of yourself.

Third, when you start each session, try to let go of all expectations. "Letting go" means that you're letting go of wanting anything to be other than exactly what it is. When you let go, you're accepting your life as it is. At that moment, you're not saying, "My life would be better if only...." You're accepting everything, the fear in your belly, the confusion in your brain, the turbulence in your body, no matter how painful or displeasing this feels. When you begin a concentration practice of any kind with the idea of "getting somewhere," or "achieving something," you'll be tempted to judge everything that happens in terms of success or failure. If you perceive one too many failures, you'll start to become discouraged, feel overwhelmed, think that you can't do it right or that it doesn't work, and then quit. In other words, when you believe that your only options are success or failure and decide that you aren't succeeding (at least not as much as you should be), you're setting yourself up to fail. Instead of succeeding or failing, you're setting out on a path—the path of "working through your test-taking anxiety." You simply can't fail at "setting out on a path," you can only have experiences along the way.

Finally, the most useful attitude you can take on as you practice these exercises is that you are going to accept your thoughts and feelings, whatever they may be. If you approach the exercises in this book with this attitude of acceptance, you won't be able to fail.

Going Up against Fear

Change isn't easy. It's taken you years to develop your fear response. You had to repeat a certain experience many times before your fearful response to it became automatic. You won't be able to completely undo this lengthy learning process in a couple of weeks, or even months. In fact, just learning to recognize when you're in a state of fear may take a long time. Becoming conscious of your fearful thoughts and feelings and then going up against your fear with awareness is a way of living, not an end in itself. You're not trying to "fix" yourself once and for all. You're learning how to explore and experience the person that you are.

Whenever you experience fear in your body and then merely consider the possibility that you don't need to let this awful feeling stop you from doing something that you want to do, you're approaching unfamiliar ground. You know what reactions you usually use to protect yourself when you are faced with a threatening situation, and, so far, they seem to have worked! However, if you go up against your habitual pattern of thoughts and actions and do something different, you just don't know what will happen. Contacting this big unknown may actually be more frightening than the thing you were originally afraid of. Paradoxically, the idea of working to become less afraid may initially make you more afraid, and your resistance to change may be high.

Changing your habitual reactions to life is how you grow. Therefore, your fear is like a big neon sign that says "walk this way." And if you walk that way, you'll learn something new about yourself, your environment, and how you interact with life. In the process you will grow. If you don't "walk this way," you will stay exactly where you are with exactly the same limitations that you have now.

So, whenever you're studying, or taking a test, or participating in class, and you notice your gut tightening up and your heart racing and your thoughts running at a million miles a minute, instead of panicking and looking for the nearest way out, sit yourself down and mutter, "Oh, good. Another opportunity to grow."

2

Relaxing in the Face
of Fear

How many times has a friend or relative said to you, "You're all wound up. You just need to relax. Go see a show or do something to take your mind off your worries"? And how many times have you gone to a show or out with friends only to find that you can't keep your attention focused on the activity you're involved in? Your mind returns over and over to the thing that is making you uptight. Do you ever manage to feel relaxed? You may erroneously decide that you are one of a rare breed who find it virtually impossible to relax. Actually, nothing could be further from the truth.

Everybody has the ability to relax. And everybody can learn to relax their body, even in the face of apparently threatening circumstances, by practicing a combination of deep breathing, muscle relaxation, and visualization exercises. By relaxing the body, you will also calm down your racing mind and your fearful feelings. You can't experience fear or anxiety when your body is completely relaxed.

You may think that's a pretty strong claim, but it's true. In 1975, Herbert Benson described how the body changes when a person practices deep relaxation. Benson observed that during what he named the "relaxation response," the heart rate, breath rate, blood pressure, skeletal muscle tension, metabolic rate, and oxygen consumption all decreased. On the other hand, alpha wave frequency, which is associated with relaxation, and skin resistance both increased. Every one of these physical conditions is exactly opposite to the conditions that anxiety and fear produce in the body. Deep relaxation and anxiety are physiological opposites.

This chapter focuses on four techniques that, when practiced regularly, will produce deep states of relaxation—either when you're at home, or out in public.

Abdominal Breathing gets more oxygen into your system by filling the voluminous lower lung area with each breath instead of only filling the shallow, upper lung area.

Progressive Muscle Relaxation teaches you how to physically relax every major muscle group in your body. By practicing this technique, you will learn how to turn a tight muscle into a relaxed muscle at will.

Shorthand Muscle Relaxation involves three abbreviated versions of Progressive Muscle Relaxation, all of which will enable you to quickly and subtly relax your body in public. These exercises will be particularly useful during examinations.

Visualization teaches you how to create and enter mental scenarios and how to short-circuit the incessant stream of anxiety-producing thoughts while enhancing a sense of peace and well-being.

By itself each method can produce a deep state of relaxation, but often two or more can be combined to deepen the relaxation experience.

Abdominal Breathing

If you've ever watched an infant breathing, you would've noticed that every time she breathed, she breathed from her abdomen. As you get older, and as stress from your daily life accumulates, the muscles in your body react to this stress by continuously holding on to a certain amount of tension. One set of muscles that commonly tenses in response to chronic stress are those located in the wall of the abdomen. If your abdominal muscles are tight, they will push against your diaphragm as it extends downward to initiate each new breath. This, in turn, inhibits the amount of air you inhale. The result is a shallow breath centered high up in the chest.

The fact that you're taking the time to read this book suggests that you're already familiar with shallow-chest breathing. It's the type of breathing you do when you're in a classroom, reading a question on a test that you don't know the answer to, while your mind repeats over and over, "I can't do this. I can't do this. I'll never be able to do this." I'll bet that the type of breaths you take when you're in this situation are shallow and located high up in your chest. This is how you breathe when you become anxious and afraid.

Often when your breaths are high and shallow, you may feel as though you aren't getting enough oxygen. Instead of responding to this lack of oxygen by taking deeper breaths, you may take shallow breaths more quickly. Eventually this rapid breath rate can lead to a state called *hyperventilation*. This means that even though you are breathing faster, the oxygen level in your body is still low because your breaths are so shallow. And, on top of that, now too much carbon dioxide starts being released from your system.

When you hyperventilate you often feel like you're not getting enough air. You may start to feel dizzy or disoriented. Your heart may begin to beat very fast. At this point, you start to try to make sense of all these scary feelings and may come to the erroneous conclusion that you are about to have a heart attack, or that you are about to lose control altogether. These thoughts can escalate your initial sense of panic into a full-blown panic attack.

The depth or shallowness of your breathing affects your physiological well-being in several ways. When you breathe deeply from your abdomen, your lungs are able to expand fully, and you're able to inhale more oxygen. This means that

- More carbon dioxide and other wastes are removed from your body because more oxygen reaches the bloodstream. (Your blood takes oxygen to each of your cells where it is exchanged for these waste products.)

- More physical energy is generated because more oxygen goes to the muscles.

- Greater clarity of mind is experienced because more oxygen reaches the brain.

Breathing from your abdomen helps you become more aware of the sensations in your body and less able to run your mind around the same thought loops that anxiety often produces. You're able to maintain a more calm emotional state. Learning to breathe from your abdomen can produce the exact physiological changes that will help you do well on a test.

Take a moment here and pay attention to the quality of your breath as it enters and leaves your body. First lie down and close your eyes. Notice whether your breath extends low into your abdomen or stays high up in your chest. An easy way to test this is to put your hand on your abdomen (just under your rib cage) and see if your hand rises and falls with each breath. Are you breathing slowly or rapidly? Do you fill your lungs with air, or do you only partially fill them? Take a few more minutes and simply feel the sensations of your breath as it enters and leaves your body.

If you think that you probably breathe shallowly a lot of the time, don't let this worry you. With a little practice, anyone can learn to take deep, full-belly breaths in most situations. After you've practiced the following exercise, you'll realize that about three minutes of deep breathing can enhance your level of calmness immensely.

Deep Breathing Exercise

1. Lie down and close your eyes. Take a moment to notice the sensations in your body, taking note of any tension. Take several breaths and see what you notice about the quality of your breathing. Where is your breath centered? Are your lungs filling all the way up? Is your chest moving when you breathe? Your abdomen? Or both?

2. Place one hand on your chest and one hand on your abdomen, right below your rib cage. As you breathe in, imagine that you are sending your breath as far down as it will go, all the way down to the lowest part of your lungs. Feel your lungs expand. As you do this, the hand on your chest should remain fairly still, but the hand on your abdomen should rise when you inhale and fall as you exhale.

3. Continue to gently breathe in and out. Let your breath find its own pace. If your breathing feels unnatural in anyway—if you feel like you're gulping air or you're holding your breath, just maintain your awareness of that sensation as you breathe in and out. Eventually, any straining or unnaturalness should ease up by itself.

4. After you have breathed mindfully for a few minutes, begin to count each time you exhale. After ten exhales, start the count over again with one. If at any time you forget the number you are on (and you will sooner or later), start over again with one. Continue this for approximately ten minutes. Your thoughts may often wander and dwell on worries or amusements. But every time you notice that you're not concentrating on the exercise, let go of whatever you're thinking, and return your attention to the exercise.

You may feel that you have so much trouble "keeping your breath regular" that the act of simply focusing on your breathing can bring up feelings of anxiety. Or it may seem like you can't just watch your breathing without feeling as if you have to manipulate it in some way. Or you may have carried tension in your abdominal muscles for so long that initially you have difficulty learning how to let your lungs completely fill up with air. At the beginning, you may feel like you're gulping air, holding your breath, or breathing unevenly. If you had difficulty with the deep breathing exercise, here are some suggestions that may make it easier:

- Increase the pressure of the hand on your abdomen. This added sensation may make it easier for you to find the place where you want to direct your breath. Some people find that the weight of a book on their belly is more helpful.

- If you take your hand off your abdomen and increase the pressure on your chest by pushing slightly harder with the hand that's still there, your breath may automatically flow down into the lower part of your lungs—the area where the pressure is now lower and resistance is less.

- If you overexhale slightly—if you push a little more air out than you would when you exhale normally—more air will automatically flow into your lungs when you inhale. You may want to try this as you press slightly on your chest at the same time. Continue breathing like this for a few minutes. This method is particularly useful if you are out in public and don't have the opportunity to lie down and focus (for instance, if you are in a classroom taking a test). It can effectively help you relax during the initial stages of panic or extreme fear.

- If you feel afraid or anxious while practicing this exercise, try to focus on what the sensation of fear feels like in your body. Where do you feel it? Your stomach? Your chest? Does it have a shape? What muscles are involved? Does your heart rate change? Your center of breathing? Can you take deep, satisfying breaths even though you feel afraid? Try to sense everything you can. If your mind is making up stories about why you feel afraid, remind yourself that these stories are fears, not the truth, and that the best thing to do is to ignore them. Keep returning your concentration to your breath and any sensations you feel in your body. If you continue to keep bringing your attention back to your breathing and your body, any fearful feelings that arise will eventually ease away.

Progressive Muscle Relaxation

You may think that the only way to counteract stressful feelings is to lessen the amount of actual stress in your life. However, there is another method. You can learn to relax your body even when it is under considerable stress regardless of what that stress may be. Remember, it's impossible to feel afraid when your body is deeply relaxed. The most effective technique for relaxing the body is Progressive Muscle Relaxation.

Progressive Muscle Relaxation, or PMR, is a systematic technique that involves tensing and relaxing all the various sets of muscles within the body in a specific sequence. It was developed in 1929 by Dr. Edmund

Jacobson. Realizing that the body responded to anxious and fearful thoughts by storing tension in the muscles, he found that this tension could be released by consciously tightening the muscles beyond their normal tension point, and then suddenly releasing that tension. By repeating this procedure with every muscle group in the body, Jacobson discovered that a deep state of relaxation could be induced.

Although Jacobson's instructions for PMR were complex and involved more than two hundred different muscle relaxation exercises, it has since been discovered that a regimen of sixteen exercises can be equally as effective when practiced daily. These exercises divide the body into four major muscle groups: the arms, the head, the midsection, and the legs.

If you practice PMR as outlined in this chapter, you will experience the physical benefits that Herbert Benson defined as the relaxation response. But, perhaps even more importantly, if you continue to regularly practice the PMR exercises for several months, you'll find that the overall anxiety in your life will gradually diminish. And as your anxiety lessens, your ability to face fear-producing situations will increase. You'll no longer see test taking as the insurmountable obstacle to your future that it may seem to be now.

As you practice PMR regularly, you'll learn how to fully enter your body and become aware of a variety of sensations that you may now be out of touch with. PMR practice will teach you:

- **Which muscles in your body store tension.** Many people have their favorites. Can you identify any groups that stay tight most of the time? Your abdominals? Stomach? Chest? Shoulders? Jaw? Once you have identified a muscle group that tends to be chronically tense, take a few moments each day to focus on the feelings in that area. Notice how these feelings change over time.

- **What actual sensations of tenseness feel like.** Often you're unaware of how your body actually feels. You may have a tendency to block out any physical sensations, putting all your attention into your thoughts.

- **How to make a tense muscle relax.**

- **How to become aware of a muscle that is beginning to tighten because you're in the early stages of stress.** Early awareness of muscle tension will clue you in to the fact that you are feeling afraid. You can then counteract your fear by practicing PMR.

- **That any sensation in your body is transitory.** Feelings can change from one moment to the next. For example, one day you're practicing PMR, and you notice that your chest feels heavy and tight. The next day it may feel more relaxed, but jumpy. The day after that it may feel clear and unobstructed. Or you may notice the feeling doesn't change from day to day, but may change right in the middle of the exercise. When you realize this, you will also realize that feelings such as fear and anger are just as impermanent and can change into something else just as easily.

Getting Ready

Find a quiet place where you won't be disturbed. You may want to use white noise—the humming of an air conditioner or fan per-haps—to cover up sounds that you have no control over. You should be wearing loose, comfortable clothing that won't bind you anywhere. If something fits more tightly than you would like, you may want to loosen a belt, or unzip a zipper. Assume a comfortable position, one in which all parts of your body are well supported. This usually means lying down, although sitting in a recliner is also fine. Extend your legs and let your arms lie easily by your sides. Close your eyes and take several deep belly breaths. Notice how your breathing slows with each breath. Feel the tension in your body begin to ease up. You are now ready to begin the exercise.

The Basic PMR Technique

When you practice the following exercises, repeat each tensing and relaxing cycle twice with each muscle group. Always tighten each group for seven seconds, and allow the muscles to relax for twenty seconds. Take deep, slow belly breaths throughout the exercise.

Be careful when you tense muscle groups in your neck and back, particularly if you often have pain in these areas. If you experience pain when contracting any muscle group, stop tensing these muscles and simply ease any tension by focusing your attention on that area. You may experience muscle cramps if you overtighten the muscles in your feet.

Arms

1. Clench both hands tightly, making them into fists. Hold the tightness for seven seconds. Put your attention on the muscles you are contracting. What does it feel like? Now, let go of the clenching. How is the feeling different after you let go? Stay focused on any sensation you experience. Let the sensation of relaxation deepen for twenty seconds. Now clench your fists again. Hold the tension for seven seconds, then relax for twenty seconds. Notice the feelings.

2. Bend both elbows and flex your biceps. Hold this "muscle pose" for seven seconds, then let out the tension. Flex a second time, and relax. Follow the sensations.

3. Tense your triceps, the muscles underneath the biceps, by straightening your arm and pushing down as hard as you can with the palm of your hand. Hold the tension, then relax. Repeat the cycle a second time.

Head

1. Lift up your eyebrows as high as you can and feel the tension in your forehead. Hold this, then suddenly let your brow drop and become smooth. Notice how the feelings differ between tensing and relaxing.

2. Squinch up your entire face, as though you were trying to fit every part of it onto your nose. Feel where the strain is. Then release the tension. Feel your face when it's absent of tension.

3. Close your eyes as tight as you can, and smile, with your mouth, closed as wide as you can. Hold it, then relax. Allow any tightness to drain away.

4. Clench your jaw, and push your tongue up to the roof of your mouth. Hold it. Notice where you feel the pressure, then release. Notice how the feeling changes.

5. Open your mouth into a big, wide *0*. Hold it. Then release your jaw so that it goes back to its normal position. Feel the relaxation and notice the difference.

6. Tilt your head back as far as you can, until it presses against the bottom of your neck. Hold it, then relax. Roll your head slowly to one shoulder, hold, and relax, then over to the other shoulder and hold, and relax. Feel which muscles are being stretched and which are being pressed against. Lift your head up to its resting position. Feel the relaxation spread down through your head, neck, and jaw. Let your mouth fall open slightly as the tension melts away.

7. Bend your head forward until your chin is resting on your chest. Notice how the muscles in the back of your neck feel as they stretch. What sensations are in your throat? Release the tension as you let your head rise up into a neutral position.

Midsection

1. Bring your shoulders up as high as you can—as though you are trying to touch your ears with them. Hold this position. Now let

them fall back down again and as you do, see if you feel a heaviness as the muscles relax.

2. Now stretch both shoulders back as though you were trying to touch your shoulder blades together. Feel which muscles are being stretched. Hold the position, then relax.

3. Bring your arms out straight from your shoulders so that they are parallel to each other. Then, while keeping them straight, cross them, making the cross as high up on your arms as you can. Feel the stretch in your upper back. Hold it. Now return your arms to your sides and notice how it feels when the muscles let go.

4. Take a deep breath and before you exhale, contract the muscles in your abdomen and stomach. Study the feelings of tension, then exhale and release the contraction.

5. Place your hand on your abdomen and inhale deeply. Let your breath push your belly up to your hand as your hand pushes back. Now exhale and focus on how it feels when the relaxation spreads through your body.

6. Gently arch your back, and pay attention to the stretch in the lower back area. Hold the tension, then lay your back flat again as you concentrate on feelings of ease and heaviness.

Legs

1. Tighten your buttocks and thighs. Increase the contraction by straightening your legs and pushing down hard through your heels. Hold this position, then let go. Notice the difference in feeling between tightening and letting go.

2. Tense your inner thigh muscles all the way down to your knees. Hold the contraction, then release it. Feel the relaxation spread down through your legs.

3. Tighten your leg muscles while pointing your toes downward. Hold it, then release, returning your toes to a neutral position.

4. Flex your toes by drawing them upward towards your face as you tighten your shin and calf muscles. Hold, and release, letting your feet hang loosely.

Finishing Touches

Now lie completely still for a few minutes. Concentrate on the feelings of ease and heaviness. Allow the sense of relaxation to fill your body. Take a few deep belly breaths. Let your lungs completely fill with each inhalation. Feel the tension drain from your body more and more with each breath.

Let your attention wander through every part of your body as it looks for tension. If there is any tension left in any muscle group, repeat the appropriate exercise and feel the sense of ease and warmth and heaviness. Just lie there for a few more minutes, and let the relaxation go deeper and deeper. Notice everything.

Guidelines for Practicing PMR

Practice Progressive Muscle Relaxation every day. Practice about twenty to thirty minutes daily whether you feel like it or not. Try to have one practice period right before you leave for the test room. As you practice PMR, you are developing a skill—the ability to relax. In the beginning, you may find that it takes you a long time to calm down and relax. However, as you continue to practice, you will learn to relax more deeply, and the relaxed state will occur more and more quickly. In order for this skill to develop, daily practice is essential.

Tighten muscle groups completely. Each time you tense a muscle group, tighten the muscles as hard as you can without straining. Hold this tension for seven seconds. You may want to make sure a clock is clearly visible to you before you begin the exercises. Otherwise, you can count off the seconds by saying, "One thousand one . . . one thousand two . . ." and so on.

Release muscle tension completely. When it is time to let go of the muscle tension, release it suddenly and as completely as you can. Then allow the relaxation to deepen for about twenty seconds. As the muscle relaxation spreads, notice how this feeling of relaxation actually feels in your body. What are the physical sensations of relaxation? How does relaxation feel different from tightness?

Repeat each tensing and relaxing cycle twice for each muscle group. If it feels as though tension still remains in a particular area, repeat the tensing/relaxing cycle for that area a third time.

Repeat relaxing phrases. As you let the relaxation sensations develop for twenty seconds, you may find it helpful to repeat relaxing suggestions to yourself, such as, "The tension is flowing out of my body," or "Let go. Let go," or "Relax, let yourself relax." Choose the phrase that has the most meaning for you.

Pay attention to physical sensations. As you progress through each muscle group, keep your attention on whatever bodily sensations you're feeling at the time. What sensations does tensing make in the body? What sensations does relaxing make in the body? How are the two different? What other sensations do you feel that are unrelated to either tensing or relaxing? Try to follow everything with your attention.

Let go of intrusive thoughts. You will soon discover that no matter how diligently you try to keep your mind on what you're feeling, it will wander off and have many thoughts that have nothing to do with relaxing. Do not interpret this to mean that you aren't doing the exercise right, that you're not able to do the exercise, or that the exercise is impossible. On the contrary, it is perfectly normal for thoughts to interrupt your concentration. When this happens, note, nonjudgmentally, that you are having a thought and then return your concentration to your bodily sensations. You may find as you begin the exercise that your thoughts come very rapidly, and that, even after you've noticed that you're thinking, it's hard to let go and return your mind to the exercise. However, as you become more relaxed, you will probably find that your thoughts will occur less frequently and will be less compelling when they do.

Throughout the exercise take deep belly breaths. You will find that your breathing will naturally become deeper and slower the more you relax. You may find it helpful to tell yourself that tension and fatigue are flowing out of your body with each exhalation—and that energy and relaxation are entering your body with each inhalation.

Use whatever method works best. The progression from one muscle group to another follows a logical sequence, and most people find that after practicing PMR a few times, they can easily remember this sequence. Even if you forget the sequence in the middle of the exercise, you will be able to continue by imagining ways of tensing each of the various muscle groups in your arms, head, midsection, and legs. Some people do prefer either to make a tape, or buy a professionally made tape of the PMR exercises. Some even like to alternate between using a tape one day and practicing from memory the next. Feel free to experiment and use whatever procedure works best for you.

Shorthand Muscle Relaxation

Although the basic PMR procedure is an excellent way to relax, it is difficult to practice it when you're out in public. It takes too long to go through all the different muscle groups to make it a practical tool for on-the-spot relaxation. And you would probably get a few strange looks when you begin the muscle contractions. In order to relax your body in a public place (such as a testing room), you need to learn one of the following Shorthand Muscle Relaxation methods. Since they are all based on the PMR technique, you will need to have practiced PMR until it feels like a natural part of your life.

Simultaneous Contraction

One way to shorten the time it takes to relax all your muscles is to contract several of the muscle groups in each of the four body areas at the same time. First, find a place where you can sit comfortably. You will want to breathe normally as you tense each muscle group. Try to start each period of relaxation with a long exhalation, but feel free to inhale when you need to. Hold each tensing for seven seconds and allow each group to relax for twenty seconds—just as you did in the PMR exercises. However, as you become more practiced, you may need less time for both the tensing and relaxing parts. Always keep your attention focused on the sensations in your body. By now you'll know how your muscles feel when they are tight and when they are relaxed. Divide the exercises up this way:

1. Make tight fists while flexing your biceps and forearms in a Charles Atlas pose. Or, if this would make you feel too conspicuous, tighten all the muscles in your arms as they remain straight by your sides. Hold the position, then relax.

2. Press your head back as far as you can. Roll it clockwise in a complete circle, then roll it once counterclockwise. As you do this, wrinkle up your face as though you were trying to make every part of it meet at your nose. Press your tongue against the roof of your mouth, tense your throat muscles, and hunch your shoulders up. Hold the position, then relax.

3. Arch your back as you take a deep breath. Hold the position, then relax. Take another deep breath, and this time push your abdomen out as you inhale. Hold the position, then relax.

4. Point your toes up towards your face while tightening your calf and shin muscles. Hold the position, then relax. Next, curl your toes while tightening your calf, thigh, and buttocks. Hold the position, then relax.

Release-Only Relaxation

Since weeks of PMR practice have made you adept at recognizing and releasing tension in your muscles, by now you may not need to deliberately contract each muscle before you relax it. Instead, scan your body for tension by running your attention over every muscle group. If you find any tightness, simply let go of it, just as you did after each contraction in the PMR exercise. Again, you need to stay focused on what you are doing and really feel the sensations. Work with each area until it feels like all the tension is gone. If you come to an area that feels tight and won't let go, tighten that one muscle or muscle group before you release the tension. You will find this method to be faster than Simultaneous Contraction. It is also a good way to relax sore muscles that you don't want to aggravate by overtensing.

Cue-Controlled Relaxation

In Cue-Controlled Relaxation you learn to relax your muscles exactly when you tell yourself to, combining a verbal suggestion with abdominal breathing. First, take a comfortable position, then relax yourself completely using the Release-Only method. Remember to focus on your belly as it moves in and out with each breath. The breaths are slow and rhythmic, and with each one you become more and more relaxed. Now, on every exhalation say to yourself the word "relax." Notice how saying "relax" makes the feelings of calmness and ease spread throughout your body. Continue this practice for five minutes, repeating the word "relax" with each exhalation.

By practicing in this way, you are teaching your body to associate the word "relax" with the feeling of relaxation. After you have practiced this technique for a while, and the association has been made, you will be able to relax your muscles anytime, anywhere, just by mentally repeating the word "relax" as you exhale and by focusing on the feelings of tightness and ease in your body.

When you practice these relaxation techniques, pay attention to which parts do and don't work for you. Nothing that has been described here is etched in stone. If a different muscle sequence feels more natural to you than the one Jacobson used, by all means try it. Or, if you find you need more or less time for either the tensing or relaxing segment, adjust the time accordingly. Remember, you are the person who best knows how to communicate with your body.

Visualization

Every day you use your imagination to create scenes—memories of past Christmases, daydreams of last night's date, visions of how you want your future to be. Everyone has the ability to use his or her mind in this way. But you may not realize that you can also use this ability to relax by mentally constructing a peaceful scene to imaginatively enter in times of stress.

A peaceful scene is an imagined setting that has several qualities you might look for in a vacation spot. Since you are the one who is making this scene up, it will be a place that you find interesting. It will be somewhere that seems restful to you. It will be a setting where you will feel safe and secure—where you'll be able to let your guard down and completely let go of all of your tension.

You may find a scene from nature to be the most relaxing place that you can imagine. Or maybe an indoor scene, one where you can lock all the doors and windows, will give you the sense of security you need to feel safe. You can visualize a place you've been to before, or one entirely made up from your imagination. Many people create an image that's some sort of combination of the two. Your peaceful scene should be calming and appealing to you. Beyond that there are no limits.

Before you begin visualizing your peaceful scene, find a comfortable position, either sitting or lying down, then take a few minutes to practice your Cue-Controlled Relaxation technique, or one of the other relaxation techniques if you prefer. Use whichever one works best for you. It is important to take enough time to become relaxed, since visualization works best when your brain is emitting alpha waves—the waves your brain makes when you are in a relaxed state.

When you feel you are relaxed, notice where your concentration is. It may be on a sensation in your body, or an object or sound completely outside of your body. Wherever it is, start to pull it in until your focus is located inside of your head, resting just behind your eyes.

Now pretend that your imagination is a friendly travel agent. Tell it that you'd like to get away for a little R and R, then patiently watch your internal viewing screen to see what it suggests. A scene may start to form in your imagination. Or, instead of an image, you may hear words—"the lake," "the beach," "Baja"—and these words may, in turn, stir an image to life. However it happens, when an image does show itself to you, don't question it. Don't ask if this is your ultimate restful scene, or if maybe another scene would appear more clearly. Accept this location or activity as one that has a peaceful resonance for you.

If a scene doesn't start to appear, choose a place or or an activity that appeals to you. Where would that be? Out in the country? The woods? A meadow? Are you in a building? A cabin? The house where you grew up? A penthouse in New York? What are the objects around you? What are their colors and shapes? What sounds do you hear? What are you doing? Are you lying down? Sailing a boat? Watching TV? Think a moment about what would seem restful to you.

Once your imagination has settled on a scene, you may find that it appears to be somewhat hazy. The shapes and colors may not be clear, or parts of the scene may actually be missing. This is perfectly normal. Don't be disappointed if your scene doesn't automatically appear in 3-D Technicolor. With a little practice, you will learn to draw out the details and make your scene become vivid.

Visualization Skills Guidelines

Visualization is a skill. Like many skills, such as painting, building a house, or doing math, some people will naturally be more adept at it than others. You may be a person who can sit down and with little practice recreate the cabin at the lake so clearly that you feel you are actually there. Or you might be someone who finds that when you close your eyes, it's difficult to see anything at all (even though you probably visualize scenes quite well when you dream). If you don't have a natural predisposition to visualization, you will be able to develop this skill with practice. The following guidelines will help you bring your visualizations to life.

Add definition. Once an image appears, you can bring out the shapes in your scene by running your mind over the outline of the images that you see, as though you were tracing them with a pencil. Try to actually see the edges of the objects getting darker as you trace them with your mind.

Add detail. If there are any gaps in your scene—places that either seem hazy, or are devoid of any image at all—put your attention on the gap and ask yourself, "What is it?" Hold your attention on the area and see if the image starts to clear. It may, or it may not. If nothing happens, that's fine. As you practice visualization, over time your scene will become more and more complete.

Enhance color. Take a look at the colors in your scene. Are they varied, or does your scene tend to be monochromatic? Are they vivid or faded? Locate the light source in your scene. How does light falling on an object affect its color? Notice the areas that are in shadow. How does the absence of light affect the colors? If you need to vivify a color, place your attention on the object (let's say it's a tree) and with each exhalation say to yourself, "I am breathing green into the leaves" (or whatever phrase is appropriate). At this point, put all your attention on the leaves and see if you can increase the color as you exhale.

Add sound. What sounds would you hear if you were actually in your scene? Are there birds? Animals? Insects? Is there water? Wind? What sounds would these elements make? Think of the last time you heard these sounds and bring that memory back into the scene you are creating.

Add scent. What does the environment smell like? The aromatic scent of pine? The dank smell of earth? The perfumed scent of jasmine?

Is someone cooking in the distance? Is there a faint scent of soap on your skin? Recreate the appropriate scents in your imagination.

Add touch. Run your hand over various objects: the ground, the bark on the tree, the rock in the sun. Does the grass feel cool? Does the sun warm your body? Is the shade of the forest cool and refreshing? Can you feel the wind blow against you? Or the warmth of the fireplace? As you sit or lie down, can you feel the pressure on the part of your body that touches the ground? The chair? The bed? Become aware of the various textures, and temperatures, and pressures that make up your scene.

Shift your viewpoint. Pay attention to the perspective from which you are viewing the scene. When you are first forming your scene and etching in the details, it will appear to you as a movie would if you were watching it. That is to say that you, the viewer, are outside the scene and are able to take in the entire view encompassed by the scene. However, after the scene has been established, you will need to shift your viewpoint from a place outside of the scene, to behind the eyes of the imagined you. For example, if you imagine that you are lying down underneath some trees, instead of seeing yourself on the ground among trees, you would instead see only the tops of trees waving in the breeze against the clear blue sky. That would be what the you in the imagined scene would be able to see. By seeing things from the perspective of the imagined you, you draw yourself completely into the image. Visualizing your scene from this perspective will make it easier to feel as though you are living the scene rather than viewing it.

Work with whatever appears. Some people report having difficulty holding an image steady in their mind. They say that their scene jumps around, or fades in and out, or won't appear at all. If this happens to you, put your attention on whatever is there. If the image is jumpy, watch the image jump. If nothing appears, concentrate on what nothing looks like. Whatever appears, watch it as intently as you can. It will change and become more clear with each attempt. Sometimes people who have trouble mentally seeing an image do much better with recreating sounds and smells. You may want to try starting with the sound of a gurgling brook, or the fragrance of a eucalyptus. A relived sound or smell might help draw the visual part of your scene out.

Practice daily for at least twenty minutes. As with any skill, your ability to visualize will improve in direct relation to the amount of time you spend practicing.

As you practice visualizing you will notice that, no matter how hard you try, your concentration will often wander from the scene you are creating to other topics that are pulling at your attention. Many of these nagging thoughts may be related to things or events in your life that make you nervous or afraid. Some may be related to other strong emotions that you've felt and continue to feel along with their accompanying thoughts. Some thoughts may be plans for the future, others may be critiques you make about others or yourself. Everybody who begins a type of concentration practice will have intruding thoughts. The number of these thoughts will diminish with practice, but you will *always* have unwanted thoughts. Whatever the content of your thoughts may be, the procedure is always the same. As soon as you notice that you're thinking about something else, here is what you should do:

1. Acknowledge, in an nonjudgmental way, that you are thinking. ("Oh, I'm having a thought.")

2. Drop the story line behind the thought, however enticing it may be. (If a certain topic keeps demanding your attention, tell yourself that you'll think about it at at a later time.)

3. Return your attention to creating your scene.

Remember: The key to relaxing through visualizing a peaceful scene is to make the scene as real as you possibly can. Use a lot of detail. Incorporate information that you would gather through three senses in addition to sight. To create a sense of reality, notice which objects are in your foreground, middle ground, and background. And finally, view the scene from the perspective of the imagined you.

Examples of Peaceful Scenes

Here are two peaceful scenes that may give you an idea of how to put your own scene together.

Nature Scene

You are walking on a path that winds up a large, wooded hill. The rutted path is strewn with roots and stones and branches. As you step over each obstacle, your breathing becomes fuller and deeper and drops low into your belly. You feel good and strong and whole, and glad to be on this adventure, ruts and all. You turn onto a narrow path, and the woods quickly become thicker, darker, more serene. The air is now strongly scented with pine and laurel, and you notice that the atmosphere has taken on a much deeper, softer stillness. Soon you come upon a large circle of very tall trees. In the middle of the circle is a thick cushion of soft, dry moss. As the sun streams through the branches, it fractures and falls dappled on the plush moss carpet. You walk toward the trees and as you step into the circle, you notice that the small pack you've been carrying has become very, very heavy, so heavy that you feel you have to sit down and rest. You drop your pack to the ground, and as it falls from your shoulders you feel an incredible lightness, as though the pack had comprised half your body weight. Suddenly you understand that this pack contains everything against which you struggle—every feeling, every pain, every thought, every tension. Everything that you do battle with daily has now fallen from your shoulders. You lie down on the cool, soft moss. Two songbirds warble in the distance. A warm wind blows up from the east, and as you listen to it rhythmically rustling the tree tops, every one of your muscles surrenders any last bit of tension. And each gust of this gentle breeze fills you with ease and peace and joy.

Indoor Scene

The weeks leading up to this day have been busy and demanding. But every time you felt overtaxed and overwhelmed, your mind would fly ahead to today's date and you'd remember, "I'm going on vacation. I'm going to go home." Now, finally, here you are, boarding a train that will soon take you to that place of supreme comfort and rest. You step aboard and follow the conductor down the long, narrow corridor. As you near the end of the car, he turns to you and says, "The train company feels that, in recognition of the trueness and goodness of your heart, you deserve its finest accommodations." As he opens the doors, you see that the entire next car has been turned into a private studio just for you. Nearest the door there is a heavy, four-poster bed with a billowy mattress and a brocade curtain you can close to create a sense of security. Next, you notice a small, but very complete kitchen beside an equally small table that can expand to accommodate, if accommodation is what is needed. Past the kitchen is a large, circular, tiled tub that's sunken down into the floor so that even if the train jerks suddenly, the water will stay exactly where it's supposed to. When you reach the end of the room, you realize that your car is the last car on the train. You see this clearly from the small observation area that is completely surrounded by glass. Underneath the glass dome there is a plush couch with two overstuffed, comfy chairs opposite it, and a coffee table in the middle, complete with your favorite magazines. You sink down into one of the chairs, toss off your shoes, and put your feet up on the table. Your eyes close for what seems like only seconds, but when they open you see the train has left the station and, outside the observation dome, an ever-receding panorama now holds you enthralled—the mountains, the trees, the snowcapped peaks, the lake shimmering in the distance. The sun has almost set and the sky is washed in purples and reds and is filled with towering red and orange clouds. And as you gaze, you become the rhythm of the wheels clacking, and feel the lull of the gentle rocking, and suddenly you know that there isn't a worry in the world that can overshadow the sense of beauty and wonder and awe that at this moment you hold in your heart.

Further Practice

How well you visualize an object depends on how well you can become completely involved with the image you see in your mind's eye. Here are a few practice exercises that will help you develop your ability to truly enter the world you are mentally creating.

Before you practice the following exercises, you need to have first worked on creating your peaceful scene, and you should be familiar with the nine guidelines in the previous section.

Take a few minutes to relax before you begin each session of Behavior Visualization. Either lie down or sit comfortably in a chair. Take several deep breaths, then scan your body for tension. Release any muscular tension that you find, then take several more deep belly breaths. Now close your eyes and focus your concentration on the area that is midway between your eyes and about half an inch up from the top of your nose. This focal point will be like a movie screen where all the images you visualize will be projected. As you watch this internal screen, let yourself become more relaxed with every breath. Now you are ready to begin.

Starting Simple

This exercise will help you develop a sense of unity with your imaginary scene, allowing you to truly "enter" it. Set an object that you like in front of you—it could be a flower, a coin, a photograph, a candle—anything that you feel draws your interest. As you gaze at this object, also explore it with each of your other senses. How does this object feel when you touch it? Perhaps different parts of it feel completely different from each other. How does it smell when you inhale? If you were to taste it, what would the taste be like?

Examine your object in this way for about a minute. Then close your eyes and as you continue to touch, smell, and listen to your object, recreate it visually in your mind. If there are places in your imagination that remain blank, momentarily open your eyes and see what the actual detail is. Continue to build your mental image in this way, adding bits and pieces of actual sensory input whenever you come up against a wall of vagueness. As your image intensifies, try to maintain this level of intensity by incorporating the information you're still receiving from your other senses. For instance, an image that is soft to the touch will also appear soft.

Exploring a Flower

Here is another exercise that will help you unite with the object of your concentration. Find a flower—preferably one that you like—and set it in front of you. Recreate the flower in your imagination using the methods described in the above exercise. Once you've established a solid picture, pretend your mind's eye is a zoom lens and zoom in so that the image of the flower becomes very large on your viewing screen.

As you continue to physically hold, touch, and smell the flower, as well as to maintain the image of the flower in your mind, notice that a small bug has crawled out onto one of the petals. Pretend that the image that you now see is from the perspective of this bug, as though your eyes are looking out of the bug's head. Imagine how the flower looks as you crawl up and down each petal, through each fold, underneath each leaf. If you get lost, open your eyes and view the real flower. Hold it up close to your face so you can better imagine what a bug's perspective would look like. Then close your eyes again and add this information to your scene.

Facing a Wall

This exercise will help you add more details to the image you visualize. Face a wall in your room. Spend a minute running your eyes over every detail of this wall. Is there anything hanging on it? What does it look like? What is it's size, color, and shape? How is it positioned on the wall? What are the relative distances of everything on the wall to everything else? Is there furniture in front of the wall? If so, notice everything about how it looks. Where is the light coming from? What does it illuminate? Where are the shadows? Is there a door anywhere? A window? How does the frame look? The knob? The hinges? Are there any blemishes? Dents? Paint peeling? Notice everything and recreate it in your imagination.

Then, when you think you are viewing this scene as clearly as you can, open your eyes and focus on the places that were inaccurate or vague. Where did you miss the detail, and what is it really? Now, close your eyes again and add this detail. Continue this process of first visualizing the wall as accurately as you can, and then opening your eyes to gather whatever details you missed until you feel confident that your recreation of the wall is complete.

Advanced Practice

Although this exercise seems more simple in nature, it isn't. The fact that you'll have no emotional connection to the object you'll be visualizing and no actual object to view when you need fuel for your imagination makes it much more difficult.

First, close your eyes. Then center your point of focus on the large screen midway between your eyes and halfway up your forehead. As you gaze at this space, allow a small ball to come into focus. Make it three dimensional by adding shadow and light. Then suggest to yourself that the sphere will take on color. As you do this, watch carefully and see what color the sphere becomes. Once you see an expression of color, try to intensify it by imaging that you are breathing more color into the sphere with each exhalation.

When you have created a fairly stable sphere in your imagination, see if you can move it from the center of your mental viewing screen into your lower belly. It may not move easily at first, but your ability to move visualized objects will improve with practice. Hold it there, then move it back up to your forehead. Next, try to move it from your forehead to a point out in space, beyond the boundaries of your body. Then, bring it back again. Hold it there, and check to see whether your image is still clear and vivid.

3

Just Because You Think It Doesn't Mean It's True

Jill has just spent a large portion of the last two weeks studying for her political science final. She studied hard and she studied well, and she feels she understands and remembers almost all of the material that was covered in class. She has just entered the test room, taken a seat, and is waiting for the instructor to hand out the tests. As she sits there, even though she feels fairly confident that she'll do well, she notices that her mind is racing a million miles a second. Since the test isn't due to start for another five minutes, she decides to watch her thoughts and write down the first ten things that pop into her mind. Jill's list of thoughts looks like this:

1. *Let's see. Can I remember that list of dates I memorized last night?*

2. *I just know that, even though I studied pretty well, the instructor will ask questions that I won't be able to remember the answers to.*

3. *Take a few deep breaths. This isn't going to be too bad.*

4. *I can't wait until this test is over. I'll feel like a huge weight has been lifted off my shoulders. I'll just go dancing out of this classroom no matter how well I think I did.*

5. *I should be able to answer all the questions correctly. If I can't, there's something wrong with me.*

6. *I only have to study for two more finals. Then I'll be able to ease up and relax for a week.*

7. *Maybe I won't be able to write fast enough to finish the test on time.*

8. *When Fran and I quizzed each other last night, we both seemed to know the material pretty well.*

9. *Maybe Greg will take me out to dinner this weekend.*

10. *If I don't do well on this test, maybe I won't do well on either of my other finals. Maybe I just don't know how to study very well.*

As you can see, even though she entered the test room fairly confidently, her thoughts reflect a hodgepodge of possibilities, plans, and ideas. Some thoughts have the effect of keeping her confidence up. Others are an attempt to foresee any potential hazards in the immediate future. And some are completely unrelated to the test at all.

This constant internal chatter is often referred to as *self-talk*. Everyone continuously engages in self-talk. It is this endless internal thought monologue that largely determines most of your moods and feelings. When your self-talk reflects your surrounding world and circumstances reasonably accurately, you respond with appropriate emotions, and so are able to live out your life fairly sanely and perform your life's tasks fairly well. However, much of your self-talk probably isn't based on the real world at all. Instead, it reflects what you hope and fear reality might be, and your emotions then behave accordingly.

Many people aren't aware of this fact. They believe that if a thought occurs to them, just the fact that it occurs means that it must be real. For instance, if you have the thought, "Marian doesn't really like me," then surely, you figure, that must mean that Marian doesn't like you. You may then start looking for further evidence that this thought is true. How did she seem at lunch the other day? Was she preoccupied? Distant? Did she speak sharply? Or you may start to wonder why she doesn't like you. Does she think you're angry with her? Does she have a good reason? Piece by piece, your thoughts start to build up the case for the thought, "Marian doesn't really like me." Soon, your thoughts may create an entire scenario, one in which Marian doesn't like you, that bears little resemblance to the actual truth.

Slanting the Facts

Most people have a vested interest in the way they want reality to be, so their viewpoint—the way they see what's in front of them—takes on a certain slant. Their thoughts express this interest, or slant, by what they pick out in the world to see, and therefore think about.

To illustrate this better, let's look at an example. Kathy and Gena were walking together down a street. As they turned the corner, a woman approached them who appeared to be homeless. She stopped right in front of them and demanded, in a very loud voice, that they give her five dollars. At this, Kathy sifted through her purse, but could find only two quarters. When she told the woman that this was all she had, the woman turned around and walked angrily away, swearing loudly as she went. The next day, Kathy and Gena met for coffee, and they rehashed this event. Gena talked about how frightening the whole thing had been. She said that she felt sure the woman was going to physically attack them. Kathy talked about how sad it was that some people have to live that way, and wondered if the woman had ever had any children. Both women had exactly the same experience, yet each one picked out different facets of the incident that she saw, or thought about.

Much of the time, your slant is about what frightens you. When you were growing up, you may have had experiences that led you to realize that the world can be a frightening or unfair place. In order to prepare yourself for the worst, you learned to keep your "danger-scouting system" on much of the time. As you look for this possible lurking danger, your overactive inner voice (self-talk) tells you that you're just about to find it, often at the most unlikely times, and in the most unlikely places. If you can foresee it, you reason, you can protect yourself. Although this danger isn't real, you believe that it is, and you react emotionally as though something awful may happen at any minute. When you're walking around with this perception, you're seeing the world in a slanted, illogical way. And your thoughts are telling you things that simply aren't true.

For example, read over the ten thoughts that Jill listed before she began her test. If you look at the content carefully, you'll see that four of these thoughts are irrational:

> 2. *I just know that, even though I studied pretty well, the instructor will ask questions that I won't be able to remember the answers to.*

Jill has no reason to believe this. It doesn't make sense that, if you study hard and feel prepared, then you won't be able to remember the answers to some of the questions. The rational statement would be: "I studied hard and feel prepared, so I should do well on the test." But Jill is preparing for the worst potential outcome. If she thinks it, the reasoning goes, then it won't take her by surprise.

> 5. *I should be able to answer all the questions correctly. If I can't, there's something wrong with me.*

The content of this thought is directly opposite Jill's first statement. She is demanding the she be perfect, and adds that if she isn't perfect, she is somehow defective. The fear is that other people will see her as less worthy because she makes mistakes. The rational view would be to realize that no one's perfect, and it's entirely normal to make mistakes.

> 7. *Maybe I won't be able to write fast enough to finish the test on time.*

There is no evidence that this thought might be true. As of yet, Jill doesn't even know how much writing will be required, or how many questions will be asked. However, in an attempt to foresee the worst, she imagines this outcome as a distinct possibility.

> 10. *If I don't do well on this test, maybe I won't do well on either of my other finals. Maybe I just don't know how to study very well.*

Obviously, even if the grade on this test turns out to be a total disaster, this one low score won't effect the grade on any other test. But Jill's mind continues to ask, "How can I prepare for the worst?"

Different Styles of Irrational Thinking

People who often experience feelings of fear and anxiety are especially prone to seeing their world in illogical and distorted ways. As they describe their world to themselves, they often slant the facts to reaffirm their false ideas about how dangerous reality is. These ideas generate and prolong the anxiety, anger, guilt, and depression that many people feel.

Distorted thinking can be categorized into several distinct thought patterns. Learning to recognize these specific styles of thinking will help you catch your own irrational thoughts as they occur, which is the key to reducing the amount and intensity of painful emotions you may experience.

Filtering

Filtering is the process of focusing on a single negative aspect of a person or situation to the exclusion of all positive aspects. When you think in this style, you are "awfulizing" your life. It is considered distorted thinking because a large portion of reality is completely ignored, while one small part is magnified way out of proportion and seen as the entire reality. This magnification forces all your attention on the awful characteristics of a person or situation while little or no thought goes to the positive attributes.

People often engage in this type of thought distortion when thinking about relationships. For instance, your date may compliment you on how wonderful, clever, and charming you are, and then ask you why you didn't like the movie that you just saw. When you get home, you find yourself thinking that he or she likes you less than before because you have such poor taste in films. Or, if an instructor criticizes a point that you discussed on your term paper, you assume that you'll be getting a bad grade for the course, even though the instructor has liked all of your work up until now. Filtering can also allow you to continuously assume that you've failed at any given point, and so gives you the impetus to stop trying.

Overgeneralization

Overgeneralization allows you to take one specific negative event in your life, and then assume that any similar future event will turn out exactly the same way. If one prospective employer doesn't hire you, you assume that no one will ever hire you. If one time you falter while speaking to a group, you then assume you'll always go blank when you're speaking in front of people. If you do poorly on one history test, you may assume that history isn't your strong suit and that you always will fail on history tests. When you think in this style, you end up putting more and more restrictions on your life.

These words indicate that you may be overgeneralizing: *all, every, never, always, no one, none,* and *everyone*—any word that conveys a sense of absoluteness. "No one will ever love me." "I'll never get through school." "I'll never get a better job." "I'll always feel this way." Such conclusions are based on a limited body of evidence that ignores many other facts you regard as true.

Overestimating

When you *overestimate* you think the odds of a possible bad thing happening are much greater than they actually are. Whenever there's an unknown outcome, you immediately envision the worst scenario, and then assume that that's the thing that will occur—even though the real probability of this disaster striking is usually low. Remember, people who become anxious often have an overactive "danger scouting system." They are always on the lookout for the next dangerous thing that might happen. When they finally do think of something bad that might happen, they quickly switch from "might happen" to "will happen." If your husband is a half hour late getting home, you assume that it's because he's been mugged and is lying in a ditch somewhere. If you're preparing for a test, you assume that no matter how hard you study, you won't be able to pass it.

Polarized Thinking

This type of thinking only recognizes the extremes in life. People who engage in *polarized thinking* see a world of all blacks and whites with little middle ground anywhere. Everything is either terrific or awful, good or bad, the best or the worst.

People who see the world in this way often construct a reality in which they must behave perfectly. If a student doesn't get an A, he then considers himself a failure. It's an A, or else it's nothing. The first time this demand of A work isn't met, this student will forget all previous As and start to see himself as someone who'll never do well in school. This type of thinker can become an emotional pendulum, swinging from success to failure, right to wrong, loved to hated. The expectation of perfection at all times can lead to harsh self-judgment, and illusions of being defeated since the expectation seems so hard to achieve.

Catastrophizing

Like overestimating, *catastrophizing* is another way one can "awfulize" a situation. In overestimating, you assume the worst thing will happen. When you catastrophize, you decide that whatever has actually happened is the worst thing that could've occurred. People who catastrophize see the situations that exist in their lives as being much worse than they actually are. A student might think that getting an F in a specific course is the worst thing that could ever happen and agonize over receiving such a grade for a long time. She doesn't realize that, when looked at as one course among many, one "F" is practically meaningless.

If you think in a catastrophic style, you amplify your initial emotional responses. Most people can cope with the disappointments that crop up in their everyday lives. But people who catastrophize see their garden variety disappointments as "the worst thing in the world" and then feel and behave accordingly.

Emotional Reasoning

When people believe that everything they feel is the truth, they are practicing the distortion called *emotional reasoning*. They draw their conclusions about life based on the content of their emotions. If they feel angry, then someone must have done something to anger them. If they are depressed, then life must be meaningless. If they feel ashamed, then they must have done something shameful.

The problem with this type of reasoning is that emotions often have little basis in reality. As noted earlier, an emotion is a combination of thoughts and the accompanying physical sensations that these thoughts produce. Therefore, if your thinking is distorted—meaning that you're putting a specific slant on how you interpret the information you receive through your senses—your emotions will then be at least somewhat off base. And your viewpoint, which is based on these emotions, may not bear too strong a relationship to reality.

Should Statements

Often in response to being criticized as children, some people develop a fixed set of rules—*should statements*—that they use to guide them through the uncertainties of life. These rules tend to be rigid and define the standards that they believe they and the rest of the world should adhere to. Any departure from these rules, by either themselves or others, is often harshly judged as wrong.

People who have developed this style of thinking often use phrases such as "I must never," "he should have," or "she should always" in order to impose their set of unreasonably high standards on themselves and others. Although other people are often and freely criticized, those who think in this way usually save their harshest criticism for themselves. Their minds are constantly seeking out how they should be, how they should appear, and how they should act. They are continuously preoccupied with how things *should* be, which puts the seemingly less pressing issues of "what I really want," and "what I really feel" on the back burner.

Sometimes using should statements is appropriate—particularly when you consider moral issues, or matters of civility. Adhering to concepts such as "I shouldn't lie to my friends" or "I must remember to thank him" is necessary in order to coexist sanely in society. However, using *shoulds* becomes problematic when they're used to force yourself and others to live up to artificially high standards.

Here is a list of common *shouldisms* that demand adherence to an unrealistic set of expectations:

I should be a perfect student (wife, husband, parent, worker, friend, and so on).

I should get As on papers and tests.

I shouldn't be tired or weak.

I should always be helpful to others.

I shouldn't make mistakes.

I should be the smartest student in class.

I should get my work done no matter what.

I shouldn't feel afraid or angry.

I shouldn't feel envious of others.

I should strive to achieve.

I should be self-sufficient.

I should be able to control my emotions.

I should be at my best all the time.

I should always be composed and serene.

I should be assertive, but not demanding.

What Is Self-Talk?

All self-talk exists just on the edge of awareness. Although you're involved in self-talk practically all the time that you're conscious, you seldom even notice it. Becoming conscious of your internal monologue requires time, patience, and a lot of practice.

In *The Anxiety & Phobia Workbook*, Edward Bourne lists several basic characteristics of self-talk that help to explain why thoughts can be so illusive:

Self-talk is automatic. You get incredibly wound up in your thoughts and reactions; trying to pin down exactly what your world is like, and exactly who you are. And in order to support these conceptions of the world that you've created, you have the same thoughts over and over again. Some of these might be:

If I can't do it well, I won't do it at all.

I don't deserve to be treated this way.

You can make me do this work, but you can't make me do it well.

She said something disrespectful to me. How can I like her now?

If I'm not always busy, I'm wasting time.

Everyone has favorite self-talk thoughts that repeatedly play themselves in his or her head. You may have wound these thoughts up so tightly with your ideas of who you actually are, that most of the time you don't even notice thinking them.

Self-talk usually occurs in telegraphic form. Most of the time you don't think in whole sentences. Instead, your mind forms a conglomeration of images and words. Thoughts of the future often run into thoughts of the past. An image of one event might bring up images of other events that may seem to be related, or may not. And one image could carry in it several thoughts all rolled up together.

For example, let's say you're in the process of taking a test, and you come across a question you don't immediately know the answer to. You have a momentary image of another test you took in which the same situation occurred. In that test, you became sidetracked and spent too much time trying to answer one question. The end result was that you didn't have time to answer the last two questions on the test. Right now you don't actually recall "being sidetracked" and "missing the last two questions" in your conscious mind—but you do notice that suddenly your heart has started to pick up its pace, and your breathing has become centered high up in your chest. You're not sure exactly why, but seemingly from out of nowhere you are feeling the initial stages of panic. Even though you don't consciously remember the low score you got on the remembered test, your unconscious mind recalls the danger, and you react to it emotionally.

Irrational self-talk always sounds like the truth. You seldom question its content. You define your world by repeating the irrational thoughts over and over to yourself many times a day. These include thoughts like:

My life is empty.

I always have to be strong.

I'll never find a job I like.

No one knows the real me.

I know he thinks I'm too pushy.

What if I never get my degree?

I'm so ugly. I know no one likes me.

The list could stretch on indefinitely.

You probably have your own favorite set of irrational thoughts that you repeat to yourself many, many times a day. These thoughts are so familiar to your way of viewing the world that you don't ever question their content. You just think them continuously and let them direct the way you feel, and the way you behave.

Irrational self-talk is a habit of mind. Most people have had certain experiences that caused them to feel certain unpleasant sensations. And, in an attempt to avoid these feelings, they develop certain concepts—self-talk—to guide them through these pitfalls. Although these concepts may be useful at the time of the experience, they seldom have the wisdom and truth needed to guide you through all the hurts and confusions that you have yet to live. Nonetheless, you repeat these concepts until the repetition becomes a habit, as though they will keep you safe in any situation.

Irrational self-talk can cause anxiety to escalate into panic. Anxiety causes physical reactions in your body. A racing heart, sweaty palms, and chest tightness are all reactions to having stress in your immediate environment. Such reactions are perfectly natural. But, when these physical sensations occur, your irrational thoughts can jump in and, through selectively remembering the past or trying to foresee danger in the future, amp up the original sensations of nervousness and anxiety.

When your irrational self-talk kicks in, you can be sure that you'll end up being more afraid than you were before these thoughts occurred. Your anxiety may even rise to the level of panic. And your attention is drawn to how your panic is affecting your body, not the thoughts that brought it on. As your irrational self-talk raises your anxiety level in each related situation throughout your life, you'll find yourself wanting to avoid that situation more and more as time goes on. Eventually you might actually stop doing whatever it was that brought on this anxiety in the first place. When you allow yourself to slip into avoidance behaviors, your life can quickly become very limited.

How Self-Talk Affects Your Emotions

Regardless of whether your thoughts are accurate or inaccurate, rational or irrational, they all affect the way you feel. Whenever you have a thought, your body reacts to that thought with a physical sensation. When you're in a benign situation thinking benign little thoughts, the physical reaction is so subtle that you might not even notice it. However, if you're experiencing fear, anger, or any other strong emotion, many groups of muscles contract in noticeable ways. You may feel tightness in your chest or in other areas. You may feel jumpy or shaky. Your heart may race, your palms may sweat, your eyes may tear. Your body can respond in a variety of ways to your thoughts.

Your feelings are your thoughts coupled with the physical sensation that your thoughts elicit. It makes sense then that changing this equation, either by altering the mental part (by having different thoughts) or the physical part (by practicing relaxation techniques or exercising), could greatly affect the emotional outcome. This means that if you replace the thought you are thinking with another thought, you'll be able to alter the feelings that you have.

Here's an example: Alan was having a lot of difficulty with one of his test questions. As he struggled to find the answer, he realized that his anxiety level had risen off of the chart. He found himself thinking, "I can't stand this anymore. I have to get out of here."

Like most people, Alan has a self-centered interest in feeling a minimum of discomfort. He tells himself that one way to alleviate this discomfort is to remove himself from the situation that is causing the stress. If he can't find another way to handle it, he might start to believe that leaving is the only way to feel better. In response to these thoughts, various muscles groups in his body will contract, and these contractions will further escalate his sense of anxiety. He may end up feeling so uncomfortable that he'll do almost anything that he believes will end these sensations. As long as he thinks that leaving the test room is the best way to stop this anxious feeling, he might just get up and do it. And then where would he be? Instead of the low grade or the average grade that he was afraid he might get, he will have no grade at all. What do you think would happen to his anxiety then?

If Alan adopts this strategy of leaving when the going gets tough in his day-to-day life (or the strategy of avoiding scary things altogether, which is a different form of exactly the same thing), he could rapidly turn into a person who does nothing new, learns nothing new, and accomplishes very little because everything (or at least the important things) seems just a little too frightening. And, in the process, Alan would learn that when he feels really anxious, he just can't count on himself. Maybe he'll do whatever thing it is that he said he'd do, but his sense of fear may be so strong that he'll back out. And, if Alan doesn't know whether he will really do what he says he'll do or not, certainly no one else will know that either.

This would be a more accurate and healthier thought for Alan to entertain:

> *Wait a minute. I can too stand it. I'm standing it right now. I just need to take a few deep breaths and concentrate on my breathing. Then I'll take that concentration and put it on each of the questions I need to answer. Maybe I'll get them right and maybe I won't. But leaving isn't going to help anything.*

The key is to move through feelings of anxiety and fear (or any emotional response, for that matter) that keep you from leading the kind of life that you would like. You need to put yourself in the situation that makes you anxious, and then just tolerate the physical sensations of fear that your thoughts are generating. Then, as you experience these sensations in your body, observe the thoughts in your mind. What is it you're telling yourself? Whatever it is, unless you're in actual physical danger, your thoughts won't be telling you the truth. These are irrational thoughts. As soon as you realize what your irrational thoughts are, you need to make an effort to change them.

But everyone is tremendously attached to self-talk. In fact, you may be reluctant to give it up, no matter how difficult it makes your life. Even after you've watched your thoughts for a while, and noticed that these thoughts really do stir up your emotions, you still won't want to stop thinking them. You are convinced that without them you wouldn't know how to navigate in a world that can be terrifying at times. It seems that if you give these thought habits up, you will leave yourself vulnerable to the dangers of life.

If you didn't have the thought "I'll never be able to do this," how could you prepare yourself, mentally and emotionally, for a potential failure?

Where Self-Talk Comes From

Whenever you find yourself holding on to a thought by returning your attention to it again and again, it is because you have a certain belief that supports the content of that thought. You believe your thoughts because your past experiences have led you to think that this is the way life is. In fact, your beliefs are so integral to your thinking process, that you often don't even recognize them as beliefs. Instead you assume that the views you hold are accurate reflections of reality.

For instance, you may believe the statement, "The only way I will ever be happy is by being in a significant relationship. Being alone is horrible." It doesn't matter that many people who are not in relationships are perfectly happy. You believe that your own happiness is dependent upon having a significant other in your life. The experiences you have had in the past have led you to reach this conclusion.

This thought, however, is just that—a thought. It's not reality itself. Tomorrow, you might think, "Gee, life is really great! What was I so miserable about?" And that, too, would just be another thought. Neither of these thoughts has any inherent meaning. The reality of your life does not depend on, nor is it related to, any thought you may have to describe it. Your life might (and probably will) turn out to be completely different from anything your thoughts either hope or fear it will be. Beliefs that don't reflect life accurately are referred to as *mistaken beliefs*.

Most people develop their belief systems when they're young. Beliefs are usually acquired in one of two ways. You either take on those beliefs that are held by your family, friends, teachers, and society, or you acquire a belief as a reaction to something that you experience. For instance, if one of your parents was consistently mean to you, you might acquire the belief, "I don't deserve to be treated well." Or, if your parents became upset with you whenever you acted out your anger, you might develop the belief, "It's bad to be angry." Or, if your parents were very critical, you may have ended up believing that it's important to be perfect in everything you do.

Once you've accepted a belief as truth, you then continuously look for instances in life that reaffirm your idea that this is how life really is. If you originally acquired the belief "I don't deserve to be treated well," you might seek out potential relationships in which somebody is likely to mistreat you. The other potential relationships might not even register as possibilities to you. Or, if you develop the belief "It's bad to be angry," you might go through life denying, to yourself and to everyone else, that you ever get angry about anything. Once you adopt any belief, it then governs which parts of the world you actually see, and which parts don't even enter your line of vision. Sometimes a belief that seems good and rational on the surface may support specific thoughts and behaviors that, in reality, are problematic.

For instance, a woman who works hard to get ahead in life does so because she believes that working hard and getting ahead is the right thing to do. Most people will look at this hard worker and say, "What an upstanding young woman she is." However, she may be working so hard that her family life suffers or she has no time for her friends.

In general, the fear, anxiety, nervousness, and anger that you experience is generated and prolonged by the content of your thoughts. And which particular thoughts you choose to have depends largely on which specific beliefs (mistaken and otherwise) you've adopted. For the most part, you may not see your thoughts and beliefs as problems until your emotions become painful and hold you back from making your life the way you want it to be. If you change your underlying belief system, you can change how you feel and act.

Identifying Your Thoughts and Beliefs

You may be completely unaware of the connection between any specific thought you're thinking and the mistaken belief that actually supports it. Although you may think that something is a little odd the third or fourth time you fall into a bad relationship, you may not realize that it's because you actually believe, "I don't deserve to be treated well." Or, if you find yourself marveling at the calmness and generosity of spirit you are exercising towards your study partner, who has shown up late once again, you might not really be aware of your belief that "It's wrong to be angry." Your beliefs often remain invisible to you. When you observe the same situations cropping up in your life over and over again, you may start to get a hint that there is an underlying belief system at work.

When you have an irrational thought, it can either be an idea that is supported by one of the beliefs you hold, or it can state the content of the actual belief itself. For example, you could have the thought:

Here comes George. He wants me to get him something at the store. I'll do it because if I don't, he might like me less.

This is, obviously, a thought. Were you to recognize the mistaken belief underlying it, you might think:

I need to please other people if I want them to like me.

Whether you're dealing with thoughts that state your mistaken beliefs or thoughts that express ideas that arise from them, it's all the same irrational self-talk. And it all needs to be challenged in exactly the same way.

First, you need to identify your self-talk—both your irrational thoughts and the mistaken beliefs that support them—and figure out what it's actually saying. Following is a list of thirty common mistaken beliefs upon which many people base the operation of their lives every day. After each belief, a corresponding sample thought that could stem from that belief is given. These sample thoughts show how any mistaken belief can manifest itself in the academic arena. Your own thoughts and beliefs may, of course, be different. Read through the list and check the beliefs that you hold as your own. Then, after you've read the sample thought, write down a specific thought that you often have in connection with each of the beliefs that you checked.

Belief:	Sample thought:
I'm powerless.	It doesn't matter how hard I study. I still won't do well on this test.
Life is a struggle.	Studying for my final is going to be murder.
If I take a risk, I'll fail.	I shouldn't have taken this class. I'm way out of my league.
If I worry enough, I'll be able to think of everything that could go wrong.	Oh no! I forgot to . . .
If I'm nervous, I won't be able to function.	What if I feel so scared that I can't remember any of the answers?
I don't have enough time.	If I fail this class, I'll never be able to take it over again.

Belief:	Sample thought:
If things are going well, danger is lurking just around the corner.	Studying seemed much too easy. I must have missed a lot.
I'm not good enough.	No matter how hard I study, I'm just not smart enough to do well on this test.
I can't calm myself down.	I'm so nervous. What if I have a heart attack?
There is something fundamentally wrong with me.	No one else seems to be as scared as I am.
If I take a risk, I'm afraid I'll succeed.	If I pass this course, I'll have to go on to graduate school and I'll never find one I like that will accept me.
I can't stand to be separated from others.	I should have studied more, but I really wanted to talk with Shirley.
What other people think of me is very important.	If I don't do well on this test, my instructor well think I'm stupid.
I feel personally threatened when I'm criticized.	The instructor said I could've done better on my report. He thinks I'm an idiot.
It's important to please others.	My parents really want me to be an architect. It's not the career I want. But I'm so afraid they will be mad at me that I'll do it anyway.
People won't like me if they see who I really am.	If I don't come off as the smartest kid in the class, none of my classmates will like me.
If I know what I want, I won't get it.	School really doesn't matter to me. I don't need to study for this test.
In order to feel good about myself, I need to accomplish as many things as I can.	Even though I have an A average, I should've done that report for extra credit.
I need to be the best at whatever I do.	If I don't get an A in this course, I might as well give up.

Belief:	Sample thought:
I can't rely on anyone for help.	Even though I was sick for a week, I won't ask John for a copy of his notes for those days; I'll just do the best I can without them.
I should never make mistakes.	I shouldn't have missed that last question. If I'd studied another hour, I probably would've gotten it.
I should never be tired.	What's wrong with me? I should've been able to study longer last night.
I'm just the way I am. I can't change.	I've never been good at science, and I know I never will be.
I am only happy when I have lots of leisure time.	I don't need to study. I'm sure I'll do okay.
It's horrible when things aren't the way I want them to be.	I didn't get into the MBA program I wanted. My life is worthless.
If there isn't someone stronger I can lean on, I'll fail.	I didn't have time to check my homework out with Pat. I'll probably get a bad grade.
The past determines the present.	I've always been an average student. I'll probably get mostly Cs this semester.
I have no control over my feelings.	I'd planned to do a lot of studying tonight, but I'm too upset.
Anger is good.	I don't care whether he fails me or not. I'm glad I told my English instructor exactly what I thought.
If I feel something, it must be true.	I feel like I'm so stupid. I'm sure I'll get a bad grade.

Challenging Your Irrational Thoughts

It is important to become aware of the content of your self-talk before it wreaks havoc in your life. Intense, emotional reactions to people and situations are the primary red flags that point to the existence of illogical thinking. Whenever you feel afraid, angry, or anxious, you need to find out if your thoughts are operating on a belief system that isn't based on reality.

Whenever intense emotions arise, try to face them. Sit down with a pen and paper and write. Ask yourself what exact thoughts you're having about your current situation. Write down every single thought that you catch. For each situation, you may end up with one thought that is causing the problem, or several. After you have identified the thoughts that are supporting your emotional upset, challenge each one with the following eight questions:

1. Do I really think this is true? Sometimes people plug into certain thoughts when if they'd stop to reflect for a moment, they'd realize the thoughts are simply untrue. Ask yourself whether, in your heart, you believe this particular recurring thought.

2. What is the evidence that this idea is true? Try to take an objective view, and ask yourself what the experiences are in your life that lead you to this conclusion.

3. What is the evidence that this idea is false? Remember, try to step outside of your emotion, and be objective when you think about this.

4. Have I had this thought, or another similar to it, in the past? The answer to this question will most likely be "Yes." Try to remember other situations in your past that brought up this line of thinking. How are they similar to the situation you are in now? How are they different? Do you remember thinking this way when you were a child?

5. How does this idea hold me back? All of your ideas influence and guide your behaviors. Does thinking this particular thought keep you from succeeding in your life in any way?

6. If I go against this idea, what is the worst thing that could happen? People do things according to what they believe. If you decided that you do believe this thought, what would happen if you went against this one belief? For instance, if you are having the thought "I really need to find this book for Jane. I want her to like me," ask yourself what's the worst thing that would happen if you didn't get this book. And when you do think of a bad thing, challenge that thought with "And what's so bad about that?" If you get an answer to this, repeat the challenge, "And what's so bad about that?" Continue repeating this question until no more answers arise.

7. If I go against this thought, what good things might happen? If you didn't hold on to this idea so tightly, what would you do that is different? And how would this affect your life?

8. What is the belief behind this idea? This question may be a little more tricky. What do you believe that would lead you to think that this recurring thought is clearly the truth? If you can figure out the belief behind the thought, you can then become aware of the recurring thought as it appears throughout your life.

Create a More Truthful Statement

Challenging your irrational thoughts in the manner just described will help to lessen the intensity of the emotions these thoughts bring on. However, it probably won't stop the thoughts from entering your mind, and you'll still react to them emotionally. When this happens, you need to substitute the irrational thought with another thought that is closer to the truth. Review your answers to the eight questions you used to challenge your irrational thought and see if you can arrive at a statement that reflects reality more accurately.

This may not be easy. You may be very attached to the story that your thoughts and beliefs weave for you. You may feel that if you let go of this story, which continuously tells you how things really are in the world, you would no longer be yourself. You may also be unsure about how to go about letting go of the contents of your thoughts. To help your mind begin to travel along these lines, try the following exercise:

1. Write down a statement that is directly opposite the irrational thought you are working with. Say it over to yourself several times.

2. Ask yourself, "What would it mean if I really believed this statement? What part of my identity would it seem like I was giving up if I didn't have my usual thought and didn't feel these emotions? How would this make me different?"

3. Say this statement over to yourself again, this time as though you really mean it. Imagine what type of person you would be if you did really mean it. How do you think you're different from this type of person?

4. Walk up to a friend or acquaintance and express this statement as though you think it's true. What is his or her reaction? Did this person notice that you weren't expressing your "real" opinion? How do you think the reaction would've differed if you'd expressed your original belief?

Jeff's Assignment

Jeff had worked all night on his English term paper. He put on the finishing touches at 9:40 A.M. and, after showering and shaving, headed off towards campus. His professor, Dr. Lambert, had told the class that the papers were due in his office no later than 10 A.M. Jeff wasn't going to make it exactly on time, but he wasn't going to miss it by much. He felt confident that he could talk Professor Lambert into stretching the rules just this once.

When he got to Professor Lambert's office, the professor was talking on the phone. Jeff waited for five minutes then decided just to leave his paper on Professor Lambert's desk. He had just walked out the door when he heard the professor's voice behind him.

"Oh, Jeff. I'll accept this paper, but I'll need to deduct a letter from the grade since it's late."

Jeff turned around to either argue or plead, he wasn't sure which, but the professor had gone back to his telephone conversation. Jeff could sense that all hope of changing the professor's mind was lost.

As he stormed down the hall, Jeff felt his anger explode in his chest and fill his entire body. "How could he?" he thought. "Who does he think he is? I was only twenty minutes late! What a jerk!"

Realizing that he wouldn't be much good for anything as long as he was this angry, Jeff decided to go for a long jog. An hour and a half later, he felt less explosive, but he could tell that it wouldn't take long for his recurring thoughts to churn the anger up to its prejog level. He decided it would be a good idea to work with his thoughts and see if he could figure out exactly what was making him so angry. With pencil and paper in hand, Jeff sat down and wrote out the thoughts that were popping up repeatedly in his mind. He wrote out the following list:

1. *It's just not fair. I tried really, really hard, and I still got screwed.*

2. *Professor Lambert was such a jerk. He could have accepted the paper if he'd wanted to. I was only twenty minutes over the wire. He must really hate me.*

3. *Now my GPA will really be messed up.*

As Jeff ran these statements through his mind, he realized that the one that produced the most anger for him was the first one. He decided to challenge it first with the eight questions. To help him stay aware of all of his answers, he wrote everything down.

1. <u>Do I really think this is true?</u>
   Yes. I believe that I tried my best, but that it didn't do any good. And that's not fair!

2. <u>What is the evidence that this idea is true?</u>
   I worked very hard, all night, trying to complete this paper. It wasn't

my fault that I didn't get it done exactly on time. I tried! Professor Lambert should have taken that into account!

3. <u>What is the evidence that this idea is false?</u>
   (Jeff found that he really didn't want to consider this question very hard. But finally, and reluctantly, he thought of something, and wrote it down.) *Well, Professor Lambert did state that there was a deadline for handing in the paper. And, he was clear about what the ramifications would be if we missed that deadline.*

4. <u>Have I had this thought, or another similar to it, in the past?</u>
   (Jeff realized that there had been many instances in his life that he had regarded as unfair. He tried to see how far he could trace it back, and realized that even in grade school fairness had been an important issue for him.) *Yes.*

5. <u>How does this idea hold me back?</u>
   Well, it makes me really angry when I think I haven't been treated fairly. When I'm that angry, it's really hard for me to focus on anything else. And sometimes, when I feel that things won't come out the way I want them to no matter what I do, I don't even try hard. The feeling I get is "What's the use?"

6. <u>If I go against this idea, what's the worst thing that could happen?</u>
   (It took Jeff a while before he could even conceive of what "going against this idea" would mean. He finally decided that it would mean just not believing the thought whenever he noticed he was thinking it. When he caught himself thinking it, he could even counter it with the question: *What did I do to contribute to the way things turned out?* He couldn't think of any negative consequences that might happen if he did this.) *Nothing.*

7. <u>If I go against this thought, what good things might happen?</u>
   I will stay emotionally more even.
   I will do my best more often.
   I will take more responsibility for the way my life goes. That means I'll feel more powerful in the end.
   (Jeff was especially proud that he figured this last one out.)

8. <u>What is the belief behind this idea?</u>
   (Jeff needed to think about this question for a long time.)
   I think the belief is that life is stacked against me. When I walk around with this attitude, I have a sort of built-in excuse for not trying. It's like sometimes I don't try very hard because I tell myself

that something'll go wrong anyway, so why bother. I can say, "Oh,
well. It's not my fault that this bad thing happened. Life is stacked
against me." But I guess a lot of the time it is my fault. I don't try
hard enough. For instance, I could've started this paper several days
earlier. But I didn't. And instead of seeing that, it feels better to
blame someone else for my error.

Jeff looked over this last paragraph several times. He'd never quite
put it all together like this before, and he promised himself that he'd
try to be more aware of thinking this way in the future. He still felt
somewhat angry at Professor Lambert, but he realized that this anger
probably wasn't justifiable. He also saw that it didn't make sense to
reignite his anger by continuously thinking about the imagined injus-
tice. So he was able to return his attention to other things. He finished
off by writing down a statement that was closer to the truth:

Well, actually this was fair. Professor Lambert stated a deadline and
what the consequences would be if we didn't meet that deadline. Even
though I was only minutes late, I was still over the deadline. It would
have been nice if Professor Lambert had given me a break. But this was
my fault for not getting my paper in on time.

Tips for Countering Irrational Self-Talk

Thinking in an irrational way is a bad habit that you learned,
usually during your childhood. Breaking the hold that your irrational
self-talk has on you requires unrelenting practice. Here is a brief outline
of the steps you'll need to follow in order to change your irrational
self-talk:

1. Watch your thoughts. People usually initiate, or prolong, fear,
anger, anxiety, and depression with their thoughts. Pay special attention
to your thoughts when you're:

Experiencing a strong emotion.
Being critical, either of yourself or others.
Feeling depressed or lethargic.

In these situations, your mind will probably be involved in some
sort of irrational thinking. Try to become aware of the content of your
thoughts before you think them.

2. Write these thoughts down. Because your thinking is fast, telegraphic, and automatic, you often remain unconscious of much of its
content. Writing your thoughts down will help to firmly plant them
in your conscious mind. It will also help you see the error in your
logic.

3. Take a break. You'll find that it's easier to work with irrational thoughts if you can first gain some emotional distance from them. The best way to do this is to change the physical sensations that your irrational thoughts are bringing up. This will, in turn, calm down your emotional reaction. You can accomplish this by:

- Relaxing your body using your favorite exercise as described in chapter 2. Practice it for fifteen minutes, or until you can feel your heart rate decrease. As this happens, you'll notice that the rate at which you're thinking will also become slower. Once you have become more relaxed, pay attention to the thoughts you're thinking. Since your thoughts are occurring more slowly, they'll probably be easier to track.

- As you notice the content of each thought, label it. For example, you might label your thought: "having a thought that life's unfair," or "having a thought that Sam doesn't like me." Then, as soon as you have labeled this thought, let the story go, and return your attention to the sensations in your body. Labeling your thoughts will help you realize that the same thought is occurring over and over.

- Take part in your favorite form of aerobic exercise. Go to the gym, ride a bike, take a walk, go swimming—or any activity you enjoy that will get you out of your head and into your body. Again, as thoughts occur, simply label them, then let the content of the thought dissolve as you return your attention to the sensation in your body.

4. Question your thoughts. After you have calmed down your nervous system somewhat, go back to the thoughts you wrote down. Write each thought at the top of a clean sheet of paper. Then challenge that thought with each of the eight questions that Jeff used to challenge his irrational thought. Remember, write everything down.

5. Write out a more truthful statement. Go over your answers to these eight questions. See if you can notice the places where your logic is off. Then try to arrive at a statement that is closer to the truth. This is very difficult. Try to be honest. If you have trouble, go back and do the exercise that was explained in the section "Create a More Truthful Statement."

4

Approaching Your Fear
Step by Step

Over the past half century, psychologists have studied how fear of certain things, people, and situations develop, even though they objectively pose no threat. Usually, you learn to feel fear because, at some time during your life, you experienced pain (either physical or psychological), and consequently those things that were around you when you felt that pain now elicit the emotion of fear. This type of emotional learning is called *conditioning*.

If a person hears a foghorn right before he has a serious auto accident, he may become conditioned to feel fear whenever he hears a foghorn. Or, if a child has a parent who strikes her whenever she makes a mistake, she may become conditioned to be afraid of making mistakes, or of people who remind her of that parent, or both. In this manner, people can become fearful of all sorts of diverse things—failure, disapproval, hospitals, dogs, darkness, being alone, insects, blood, taking tests. People can learn to attach almost anything to their fear. When a fear becomes habitual in a person's life, this is a *conditioned response*.

One of the most effective methods of teaching people to challenge their fear was developed by a psychologist named Joseph Wolpe. He used this method, called *Systematic Desensitization therapy*, to teach his clients to respond to what they feared with something that was totally incompatible with feeling fear. Wolpe surmised that if he could induce a state of deep mental and physical relaxation in a client (a state in which it is impossible to be afraid) and then expose that client to a "small dose" of the thing that was feared, that person would then learn how to neurologically respond to that fearful thing with calmness. Wolpe introduced the fearful object, not in reality, but through the person's imagination. He found that the emotional response to the imagined situation was similar to that of the real life situation. This enabled a wide variety of objects to be used in carefully controlled amounts throughout the therapy. When a client could imagine the frightening thing in a completely relaxed state, he or she found it impossible to be anxious. After repeating this experience numerous times in the therapy room, the client's real life fear-producing situation became as unthreatening as the imagined one had become during therapy.

Wolpe found that if the fearful thing were initially imagined at its most intense, the person he was treating would find it difficult to reach a state of total relaxation. Accordingly, he devised a technique of introducing the fearful thing a little bit at a time. He had his clients construct an *anxiety hierarchy*. This hierarchy listed all the situations that related to the person's general fear and then arranged these situations from least frightening to most frightening. The person would start the therapy by imagining the least threatening scene until he or she felt no fear while viewing it. The client would then go on to a scene a little more threatening and imagine it until he or she felt no fearful response. Wolpe had his clients continue up the hierarchy until they finally reached the scene they were most afraid of. By this time, working with the scenes lower on the hierarchy had lessened the amount of fear that this final scene initially produced. This most fearful scene had already lost a lot of its power and by now seemed no more frightening than some of the earlier scenes had seemed.

Wolpe's desensitization therapy has become one of the most common techniques used by behavioral therapists to reduce levels of anxiety. But, it also is particularly suited to be used as a self-help technique. The therapist's role during the therapy is largely one of assistant. The therapist explains the method, teaches relaxation techniques, and tells the client how to proceed through the anxiety hierarchy. The client constructs the hierarchy, does the work, and determines the progress. In other words, once you understand the method, you can obtain the same results on your own that you would in a therapist's office.

If you practice Systematic Desensitization as outlined in this chapter, you'll learn how to lower what seems to be a debilitating level of anxiety to a level that will not hinder your performance in the classroom (or in many other situations that may make you feel anxious). However, while it is effective, Systematic Desensitization isn't a quick fix and requires a certain amount of preparation. Before you begin your desensitization session, you will need to first:

1. Master a relaxation technique well enough so that you can relax all the major muscle groups in your body. As you work with the relaxation exercises described in chapter 2, you'll discover that practicing deep breathing with Progressive Muscle Relaxation can rapidly produce a feeling of calm and well-being, even when you feel anxious to begin with.

2. Make your anxiety hierarchy. Figure out exactly which parts of the test-taking process you find anxiety provoking. Then rank these test-taking aspects according to the amount of anxiety they make you feel.

3. Consider which truthful statements or "coping thoughts" you will use to counter your anxiety as it rises. These are thoughts that you'll repeat to yourself while you visualize the scenes in your hierarchy.

After you complete this prep work, you'll need to recreate each scene in your imagination, over and over, until the anxiety you feel about that scene completely disappears. By alternating scenes that make you anxious with exercises that make you relaxed, you will learn to approach this fearful situation knowing you can cope with anything that comes up. Your ability to walk into a classroom and take control of the situation, rather than let your anxiety run the show, will grow tremendously.

Learn to Relax

You may go through life having little awareness of how your body actually feels, or what muscles in your body store tension and stress. When you practice the relaxation exercises in chapter 2, you'll learn to train your awareness of the sensations in your body, to recognize how the sensations change when you are anxious, and to notice where you are breathing into the body—whether it's a low, relaxing breath into the abdomen or a high, tight breath into the chest.

Before you start working with your hierarchy, you need to practice the Progressive Muscle Relaxation exercises, in chapter 2, and learn the short version well enough so that you can deeply relax the major muscle groups in your body. You also need to be familiar with the Abdominal Breathing Technique and be able to drop your breath from high chest breaths to low belly breaths at will. When combined, these two techniques are a powerful way to induce a relaxed state. Practice these relaxation techniques until you are able to completely relax yourself within ten minutes.

Finally, you need to develop your peaceful scene. While Progressive Muscle Relaxation helps to unwind your muscles once they have been tensed, visualizing a peaceful scene can give you a sense of overall well-being that may actually inhibit the formation of anxious thoughts before they occur. In your desensitization sessions, you will alternate between imagining a scene that gives you a degree of anxiety and your peaceful scene, which will help you let go of the fear that you feel.

To create your peaceful scene follow the guidelines as outlined in chapter 2. Many people find that visualizing scenes that take place in natural settings are most refreshing and rejuvenating. However, others need the kind of safety and security that only a room can offer. Whatever the subject matter of your peaceful scene may be, it needs to be interesting enough to you to completely absorb your attention. Make up a scene that best speaks to your personality (see examples in chapter 2).

Systematic Desensitization: The Method

Construct a Hierarchy

You'll need to construct a hierarchy of test-taking scenes that will progressively increase your anxiety as you imagine each one. Working with a hierarchy will let you approach your fear slowly through a series of measured steps of anxiety. Many people find that the simple act of constructing a hierarchy increases their understanding of their problem and helps them to clarify the possible reasons they experience so much fear in the test-taking arena. Breaking their problem down in this way makes it easier to see what specific things bring on their anxiety and how these things relate to other fear-provoking situations in their lives.

Constructing your hierarchy is one of the most important steps in the Systematic Desensitization process, and you need to take the time to make it accurate and complete. There are three steps to constructing your hierarchy:

1. Make a list of every scene you can think of related to test taking that might give you any amount of anxiety if you were actually living it. Try to imagine at least ten situations. Your list will include some situations you find very frightening, some that hardly affect you at all, and some that are in between.

2. Rank these scenes from least upsetting to most upsetting. As you read through each one, imagine what it would be like (or actually was like) to live through each of these experiences.

3. Choose and arrange the scenes for your final hierarchy. Your anxiety should rise from scene to scene in small steps, starting from the least threatening scene and progressing to the one that elicits the most fear. This will mean that every time you finish working with a scene, the next scene won't be much harder. Your final hierarchy should consist of at least ten to twenty scenes.

When you actually begin your Systematic Desensitization sessions, you may find that you need to change your hierarchy in some way. You may need to add a different scene, or combine two scenes, or break down one scene into two items on the list. Many people find that as they progress through their hierarchy, certain modifications do need to be made. Feel free to make alterations as you work through each scene.

Step One: Making Your List

Imagine encountering the activity of test taking in a mild, almost unthreatening way. Perhaps you hear that a friend of yours is going to be taking an important test. Maybe you walk by a classroom where you'll be taking a test in the future. Or maybe you're watching a movie in which the main character is taking a test. When you imagine these scenes, you should feel almost no anxiety at all.

Next, imagine a scene related to test taking that would elicit the most anxiety that you have ever felt while taking a test. Perhaps you're in the middle of an important test when you look at the clock and discover that only five minutes are left. Or maybe the night before the test is your most challenging time. Whatever it is, write it down.

Take some time to think about all the scenes that would fall somewhere in between these two in terms of intensity. For example, perhaps opening a book on which you will be tested makes your heart race; write it down. Or maybe driving to the test site makes you break out in a sweat; write it down. If other students finish the test before you've started the last section, does your heart start to flutter? Write it down. When you are finished your list should span the whole range of anxiety-provoking scenes related to taking a test.

A sample list of test-taking scenes for an upcoming history class might look like this:

1. *Thinking about a history test the night before the exam*

2. *Trying to answer the sample questions at the end of a chapter in a history book*

3. *Walking by the classroom where I'll be taking the history test*

4. *Passing my history teacher in the hall*

5. Listening to a lecture that covers material I haven't read yet

6. Realizing I need to finish this class in order to graduate at the end of the year

7. Being given a quiz in class that won't be counted on my final grade

8. Opening a book to study for a history test

9. Looking at pages in a history book

10. Talking to a friend who took a history test yesterday

11. Reading material in the history text that I don't understand a week before the test

12. Not knowing an answer in the middle of a history test

13. Seeing many students leave the classroom because they're finished while I still have two sections of the test left to complete

14. Listening to a friend explain a political theory that I don't understand

15. Walking into a history class

16. Thinking about a history test one week before the exam

17. Being asked to explain a political theory that I don't understand in class

18. Walking up to turn my test in and realizing that I missed an entire page of questions

19. Buying a history book

20. Asking the instructor to explain the ramifications of a particular historical event

21. Sitting in history class waiting for the instructor to arrive

22. Being asked to explain my answer on a quiz

23. Thinking about taking a test five minutes before the test is handed out

24. Being handed a history test and seeing four full pages of questions

25. Being given a lengthy homework assignment that is due the next time the class meets

Step Two: Rank Your Scenarios

Since fear is a subjective experience, it is difficult to communicate the exact amount of fear that a person is feeling. For example, if two people who have been through a frightening experience are asked how afraid they feel, both might answer, "Very afraid." But if their pulse rate, blood pressure, and skin resistance are measured, you might see that the amount of arousal was different in each person.

Behavioral therapists have set up a rating system that measures anxiety in *subjective units of distress,* or SUDs. Total relaxation represents 0 SUDs, while 100 SUDs represents the most fear you have ever experienced. All other levels of fear will fall between 0 and 100 SUDs. You will give each of your scenes a SUDs score based on your subjective impression of where your level of fear falls in relation to your most relaxed or most anxious states. As you go through your list of scenes, compare the feeling each scene would elicit with total relaxation and total panic.

For example, pretend that "Being handed a history test and seeing four full pages of questions" ranks 100 SUDs on your hierarchy. "Thinking about a history test one week before the test" might rank in the 41 to 60 range, while "Looking at pages in your history book" might rank in the 11 to 20 range. Remember, you are the expert on how you would feel in each situation. Only you can decide where each fear-provoking scene fits in relation to the others.

Since the purpose of constructing a hierarchy is to help you approach your fear gradually, it is important that approximately the same number of SUDs separates each rung of the hierarchy. If your hierarchy consists of ten threatening scenes, it would be best to separate each item by increments of about ten SUDs. In that way, you will be able to progress evenly up the ladder.

On the next page is an anxiety scale that describes the symptoms that different SUDs levels of anxiety may produce. Each has a corresponding SUDs number or range of numbers.

When using this scale to identify different levels of anxiety, pay special attention to the 41–60 range. This range is the cutoff point between feeling nervous but able to handle it and feeling afraid and not sure whether you can stay in control. It's this fear of losing control that can make your garden-variety fear mushroom into a complete panic attack. If you practice becoming aware of level 61 when you feel anxious, you can learn to avert panic by developing and using your coping thoughts and practicing your relaxation skills. This method will work both in your desensitization sessions and in the actual face of the fearful event.

Step Three: Create Your Final Hierarchy

After you've completed your list, go through it and pick out the least anxiety-producing scene and the most anxiety-producing scene.

SUDs Levels	Symptoms
0	No anxiety at all, calmness
1–10	Very slight anxiety
11–20	Mild anxiety, feeling nervous, butterflies in stomach
21–40	Moderate anxiety, feeling uncomfortable but still in control, heart starting to beat faster
41–60	Marked anxiety, heart beating fast, muscles tight, feeling uncomfortable; in control, but unsure whether you will be able to stay in control
61–80	Severe anxiety, symptoms feel as though they are intolerable, feeling of dizziness or spaciness, compulsion to escape
81–99	Moderate to major panic attack, feeling out of control, disoriented and detached; heart palpitations and difficulty breathing
100	Major panic, terror, fear of going crazy or dying

The scariest scene doesn't need to be ranked at 100 SUDs (remember, 100 SUDs represents the most fear you have ever felt, a level that might be higher than the amount of anxiety taking a test elicits for you), but it will measure fairly high on the anxiety scale. Next, make a list of your midrange scenes (41–60 SUDs). These are the scenes that would make you feel as though you were in danger of losing control. Then find the scenes that fall under 41 and the ones that fall over 60.

Starting with your least frightening scene and ending with your most frightening scene, choose ten or more scenes from your list and arrange them in 5 to 10 SUDs increments as the potential fear rises progressively from one scene to the next. Your final hierarchy might look something like the list on the next page.

Creating Intermediate Scenes

You may have difficulty creating the appropriate increment of anxiety from one scene to the next. You may find it quite possible to

SUDs Levels	Scenes
5	Buying a history book
10	Sitting in history class waiting for the instructor to arrive
20	Talking to a friend who took a history test last week
30	Looking at pages in your history book
40	Trying to answer the sample questions at the end of a chapter in your history book
50	Thinking about the history test one week before the exam
60	Thinking about a history test the night before the exam
65	Being handed a history test and seeing four full pages of questions
70	Not knowing the answer to a question in the middle of a history test
80	Seeing many students leave the classroom because they are finished while you still have two sections of the test left to complete
85	Walking up to your instructor to hand your test in and suddenly realizing that you missed an entire page of questions

relax after visualizing one scene, but be caught in the throes of anxiety when you try to visualize the one after it. The way to solve this problem is to create an intermediate scene. You can either invent a new scene with a SUDs level that naturally falls between those of the two original scenes, or you can take one of your original scenes and increase or decrease its anxiety potential. There are several ways to alter a scene to make your anxiety go up or down. For instance, the upcoming test could get closer or farther away in time:

Thinking about a test one day before the exam

Thinking about a test five minutes before the exam

It could get closer or farther away in space:

Getting in the car to drive to the exam

Being only one block from the exam site

The test could increase or decrease according to importance:

Thinking of taking an English test halfway into the semester

Thinking of taking the Ph.D. orals

Or the subject of the test could become more or less difficult:

Thinking of taking a history test (a subject in which you do well)

Thinking of taking a math test (a subject with which you struggle)

You can probably think of other variables. The point is that each scene need not be completely separate and distinct from the other scenes. When you need to create an intermediate scene, you can take the preceding or following scene and augment one of the key descriptive factors.

Coping Thoughts

A large part of your test-taking fear is created by the negative thoughts that your brain is telling you about the way that you feel (the role your thoughts play in how you feel is discussed thoroughly in chapter 3). Once you are able to recognize these thoughts as the habitual babble that they really are, you will be able to respond to them with coping thoughts—true statements that counter the automatic negative thoughts your mind produces in a fearful situation. Using coping thoughts can help you loosen up the control your fear has over you, both in your desensitization sessions and in the classroom.

Most of your negative thoughts will be variations on one theme, regardless of what fearful or anxiety-provoking situation you are in. Often, only the details change from situation to situation. Here is an example of a common thought pattern:

Part one: I am so _____ (nervous, spacey, tired, afraid, unprepared, and so on)

Part two: that I won't be able to _____ (in this case it's "do well on this test")

Part three: and then _____ (dire consequences) will happen

Once you recognize the pattern, you don't need to look any further for truth in the content. It's just a habitual way of thinking. Switch it off. You can accomplish this by having a few strategic coping thoughts firmly in mind when you enter the classroom.

Here are some sample coping thoughts. Choose two or three that are meaningful to you, or make up your own. Then memorize them or write them down on an index card. As you feel your anxiety start to mount when you are visualizing your threatening scene or when you are taking a test, repeat a coping thought over and over until your level of panic starts to drop. Or you may want to interweave one coping thought with another. See what works best for you. If at any time these statements lose their meaning, try different ones.

Sample Coping Thoughts

I can feel anxious and think at the same time.

This is only anxiety—I've been through this before.

I can practice my relaxation exercises and relax.

Just breathe and relax.

Everything is going to be okay.

I can do well on this test even though I feel afraid.

Take it slowly, one step at a time.

I can get through this.

I have time. I don't need to rush.

If I stop thinking I'm scared, I won't be scared.

These thoughts seem real, but I know better.

This anxiety will lessen—I can wait it out.

This feeling isn't dangerous—I'll be all right.

Fighting this feeling isn't going to help, so I'll just let it pass.

I can ease this anxiety by taking deep belly breaths.

If I breathe deeply, I can keep my mind on the task.

Lots of people feel this way when they take tests. I'm not the only one.

I can do it. I've done well on tests before.

All I can do is my best.

I don't have to have these fearful thoughts. I can choose to have a more realistic view.

Putting It All Together

Now you're ready to start your Systematic Desensitization sessions. When you practice this two-part technique, you will alternate imagined scenes that create states of anxiety with exercises that create states of relaxation. In this way you'll learn how to relax in the presence of that which you find frightening.

Find a place where you can sit or lie comfortably for an uninterrupted stretch of time. Have your written hierarchy nearby, and a card or piece of paper with a few of your favorite coping thoughts on it. Then follow the steps outlined below.

1. Relax. Take a couple of minutes to really settle in and unwind. Let your breath drop deep into your belly. A hand pressing gently on the middle of your chest will help your breath drop to the lower part of your abdomen. Bring your awareness to the sensations in your body. When thoughts arise notice them, then return your attention to the rising and falling of your abdominal wall. Now, begin practicing one of the relaxation techniques you worked on in chapter 2 and continue this until you feel completely relaxed—for about ten minutes. Remember, relaxing on cue is a very learnable skill, and your ability to do this will increase with practice.

2. Build your peaceful scene. As you become progressively more relaxed, allow your mind to start building your peaceful scene (see chapter 2). Make it as vivid as you can by incorporating information gathered from all five senses. As thoughts arise, notice them, then return your attention to the relaxing image you have created. Do this for a couple of minutes.

3. Create the first scene in your hierarchy. Allow the first scene in your hierarchy to appear. Try to create the scene with as much detail as you can. Make the colors bright, the shapes distinct. Ask yourself what sounds and smells are there. Recreate this scene for about a minute while noticing whether your bodily sensations change as you view the scene. Does the feeling change in your chest? Your stomach? Your shoulder? Your abdomen? Pay attention to where your body feels anxiety and what that sensation actually is.

4. Say your coping thoughts. As you maintain your awareness of this scene from your hierarchy and feel the anxiety that it causes, breathe abdominally as you start saying one of your coping thoughts over and over to yourself. For example, you might want to repeat, "You're okay. Relax now. Just relax." As you say it, make sure you're focused on what your coping thought actually means. Notice how this thought affects the feelings of anxiety in your body. Do you feel calmer?

Is the tension in your muscles easing up? Can you visualize yourself as someone who is able to cope in this fearful situation?

5. Go back to your peaceful scene. As soon as you have really felt your anxiety, return your imagination to your peaceful scene. Recreate the sense of safety and well-being you experienced there before. You may also want to practice Shorthand Muscle Relaxation (see chapter 2). Stay here until any feelings of anxiety brought about from working on your hierarchy dissolve into ease. Then return to the scene from the hierarchy. Notice whether the level of anxiety is the same as the first time. Then go back to your peaceful scene.

6. Progress up the hierarchy. Continue to alternate this first scene in your hierarchy with images and exercises that allow you to relax. When you're able to enter this first scene and experience no sense of anxiety, progress to the second scene. Work with each scene in your hierarchy as you did with the first. Do not go on to the next scene until visualizing the one before it produces no anxiety at all.

Practice Systematic Desensitization for about twenty to thirty minutes each day. Working within this time frame, you'll probably be able to desensitize yourself to between one and three scenes daily. Begin each session with the last step you successfully completed during the previous session. Work with this scene again until you are able to visualize it without any anxiety. Then go on to the next item on your hierarchy.

A Word about Completing Each Scene

It is important to finish each scene before you move on to the next one. You need to be able to feel completely relaxed while you vividly recreate a scenario—as relaxed as you would be if you were practicing one of the relaxation exercises. Even if you only feel a slight

---

Remember: It is important to progress up the hierarchy in graduated, well-measured steps. If at any time you enter a scene and feel that the SUD level is above 61—that your anxiety is so great you feel as though you might lose control—do not stay there. Re-enter your peaceful scene and practice your relaxation techniques. You'll need to step up to this scene gradually by constructing one or more intermediate scenes. Or you may want to place that scene further along in your hierarchy. Experiment and see what works best.

bit of tension or nervousness, the desensitization will not be complete. This means that your ability to stay relaxed while preparing for and taking tests won't carry over into real life. You need to repeat each step on your hierarchy until you feel no anxiety when you view it.

Each time you work through a scene on your hierarchy, you have progressed toward lowering your test-taking anxiety to a manageable level. The true test, of course, is finding out if your newfound ability to relax transfers over into the real life test-taking situation. Most people find that, once they have desensitized themselves to a scene on their hierarchy, it takes a bit more time—a few days to a few weeks—before they can experience this sense of calmness in real life. However, if after a few weeks you notice no difference in the amount of anxiety you feel about the corresponding real life situations, you may not be desensitizing completely to each scene. You may need to backtrack and redo several scenes, making sure that the desensitization process is complete. Practicing the relaxation exercises by themselves may also help.

A majority of people who work with this desensitization process improve significantly in their ability to function in those situations that once made them anxious. For most, this improvement is lasting. However, if you experience a recurrence of symptoms, go through this process again.

Sam's Story

After working ten years as a computer analyst, Samuel Beck decided to go back to school and take night classes in order to earn his MBA. Although he had always been a good student in college, he couldn't shake the feeling that ten years in the workforce had left him with a rusty set of study skills. As he studied for his statistics midterm, he was never quite sure he was memorizing the material that would actually be on the test. He also felt like he was wasting a lot of time on inconsequential things and never getting around to the important topics.

It turned out that the midterm completely justified his misgivings. Sitting in the classroom on the day of the test, he realized his stomach was turning over and cramping up. "Oh great!" he thought. "On top of everything, I must be coming down with the flu. That's all I need now." Then the professor handed Sam the test, and he turned it over, read the first question, and completely panicked. He didn't know the answer! Suddenly, his heart was racing and beads of sweat formed on his brow. He felt very, very dizzy.

Sam would have walked out of the room right then if he thought he could have made it out the door. But he knew that if he stood up, he would have ended up sprawled out on the floor, unconscious. Instead, he sat and eyed the words in front of him. He knew that he had studied the answer to question 3. What was it? He filled in the questions as best he could, but when he had finished there were a lot of blank spaces left, questions he knew that he should have been able to answer.

Sam did manage to pass the test, but not by much. And now the date of the final was approaching. He had to do better. He just had to. Or else give up the dream of getting his master's in a field he really wanted to work in.

Sam did some research. He discovered that many people had his problem and that there were several effective methods for countering test-taking anxiety. He decided that Systematic Desensitization made the most sense to him, although he did have a few reservations. "This may help some people," he thought, "but I bet it won't work on me." Nonetheless, he followed the directions and worked on developing the relaxation skills suggested. He created and wrote down his hierarchy of anxious scenes and then thought about what coping thoughts would help calm him if he actually did manage to feel any anxiety. Then he was ready to begin the desensitization sessions.

Sam began by lying down comfortably in a place where he would not be disturbed. Closing his eyes, he started practicing the PMR exercise, beginning with the muscles in his right foot. It went well at first, but after a minute or so Sam noticed he was having trouble keeping his mind on the exercise. Random thoughts kept popping up— thoughts about his work, the kids, life in general. "This can't be the way it's supposed to go," Sam thought. But he persevered and returned his thoughts to the PMR exercise every time they strayed off to something else.

He finished the PMR progression, after many "thought interruptions." His body now felt somewhat more relaxed than it had felt when he had first lain down, but he wasn't really sure he was "completely" relaxed—relaxed enough to enter the visualizations. One of his coping thoughts sprung to mind and he lay quietly for a moment saying, "Just relax. Let go. Let it all go." This seemed to deepen the relaxation level a little, and Sam then began to construct his peaceful scene.

His first reaction here was surprise. Instead of the cool, relaxing pool he was trying to see, he saw a sort of hazy, indistinct scene with a vaguely shaped tree, the water, and a lot of space he had difficulty filling in with his imagination. He worked for a while on sharpening the image and making the colors more vivid and also made a mental note to try a few visualization exercises later that day. After really working for two minutes on trying to create his peaceful scene, Sam shifted his awareness to the first scene in his hierarchy. Here the images seemed a little sharper, more defined. He went over the scene in his mind, trying to bring in other sensory information—the sound of chalk on the blackboard, the clank of the radiator, the texture of the paper. His mind continued to veer off onto other tracks, but when he noticed it wandering, he gently redirected it back to the scene in his hierarchy.

As he visualized this classroom scene, Sam noticed that he actually had become slightly more anxious than when he started. His heart was now beating a little faster, and his breathing had crept up into his chest. "Excellent," he thought. He knew the next step was to bring up the coping thought he had decided to use, but try as he might, the thought that he wanted to insert eluded him. While he searched for his coping thought, Sam's anxiety started to rise again. He realized this, let go of his effort, and almost immediately heard the words "Relax, just relax. You're okay now" echo in his mind. His anxiety then began to level off.

Here Sam shifted his attention back to his peaceful scene. This time the trees and the pool seemed more clear, more present. He consciously tried to brighten the colors, sharpen the shapes, bring in the sounds, smells, and tactile sensations. Although he still wasn't sure that he was as relaxed as he should be, this time the relaxation came more quickly. "Maybe this will work," he thought, then noted the thought and returned his attention to the pool and the trees in his imagination.

Sam alternated two more times between his peaceful scene and the scene from his hierarchy. Each time he went to either scene he was able to recreate it more vividly. By the third time he imagined the scene from his hierarchy, all his anxiety about the event was gone. Sam suddenly understood how the process worked and almost looked forward to progressing through the rest of the hierarchical scenes. However, at that moment all he felt was tired, and he decided to stop this session for the day. The whole thing had taken twenty-five minutes.

Sam continued to do the desensitization sessions daily. He found that a comfortable rate of progression involved working through one scene of his hierarchy per day. Each day, he did his relaxation exercises and then started with the hierarchical scene that he had successfully entered, without anxiety, the day before. He usually found he was still able to enter it without anxiety. If this first scene did make him anxious, he worked on it until his anxiety disappeared before he brought up a new scene. He noticed that he was able to relax more quickly and visualize more vividly every day. His thoughts quieted down more quickly over time.

He proceeded through his various hierarchical scenes without incident until the seventh day, shortly after he'd started to work on the seventh scene. As he began to imagine this situation, he was amazed to notice that his heart was beating very fast. His muscles were tight, and sweat was now streaming from his brow. He felt much more anxious than he had on any of the previous days. As he considered his extreme reaction, he decided that his anxiety level must be above 61 SUDs and that maybe he had better not try to work with that scene that day. He went back to his peaceful scene and then took a little more time and worked through the PMR sequence. Later in the day, he sat down and constructed an intermediate step between yesterday's hierarchical scene and the one he had attempted earlier that day. The intermediate step worked well and he completed the rest of the sessions without incident.

Tips for Successful Systematic Desensitization

In order to get the most out of Systematic Desensitization sessions, remember the following suggestions:

Take it slowly. As you begin your sessions, you will be learning brand new skills that will continue to develop as you practice. Take it slowly at first. Start with sessions no longer than fifteen minutes. As your relaxation and visualization abilities increase, you can lengthen the sessions to about thirty minutes each day.

You can develop relaxation skills with practice. As in other areas of life, people differ in their ability to both visualize and relax on cue. Some are more talented in one of these areas, while others find both extremely challenging. If you're a person who finds any of the Systematic Desensitization exercises difficult, don't despair. Take some extra time and practice the techniques that this exercise uses:

- If relaxation doesn't come easily to you, practice the relaxation exercises separately until you feel comfortable with them. When you use these exercises in the actual session, feel free to extend the length of time you use to relax.

- If you have trouble visualizing, take some time to practice the exercises suggested in chapter 2. Remember, it is very important to make each scene as real as you can by imagining the information and sensations that could be obtained by all five of your senses. With practice, these abilities will get better, even if it seems hopeless at the outset.

Practice the exercises every day. Learning imagery techniques is like building a muscle. In order to develop an effective imagery "muscle," you need to practice for twenty to thirty minutes daily. Even a ten-minute session is more beneficial than no session at all.

Pay attention to your physical sensations. If during a Systematic Desensitization session you begin to have an overly strong emotional response, whether it is fear, anger, or just plain boredom, stop the desensitization exercise and pay attention to how the emotion feels. For instance, if you are feeling fearful, pay attention to how the fear feels in the body. Where is it? In the chest? The belly? The neck? Where is your breathing? Does the feeling have a size? A shape? A color? Take a moment to notice as much as you can about the feeling. Then gently start the Abdominal Breathing exercise and imagine your peaceful scene. You may then choose to repeat the scene, or to end the session and make an intermediate scene before you continue.

Watch your thoughts. When doing the Systematic Desensitization exercises, or any other activity in your life that requires concentration, you will have many thoughts that creep in from your daily life. This is quite natural. Trying to suppress these thoughts would be very frustrating and might even increase your anxiety. Instead, when outside thoughts arise, notice that the thought is there, then gently return your mind to the task at hand. You may even want to label the thought: "having a thought about making dinner," or "having a thought that this won't work." If a certain topic continues to persistently come up, tell yourself that you will think about this matter as soon as you've finished these exercises. Then return your attention to what you are doing.

Work through all scenes. If a scene in your hierarchy doesn't elicit an emotional response, complete the entire visualization/relaxation sequence as though it did. It is important to subconsciously make the association between relaxation and any test-taking scenario that you may find anxiety provoking. In other words, the process may still be working even though your emotions aren't involved.

Track the anxiety gradient of your hierarchy. Ask yourself questions like: Do I feel anxious each time I visualize a different scene? Are there several scenes in a row that haven't made me anxious at all? Is there one scene where the anxiety just doesn't diminish no matter how often I imagine it? If your answer is "yes" to any of these, you may want to even out the anxiety continuum of your hierarchy in one of three ways:

- Increase the amount of anxiety that some scenes elicit.

- Decrease the amount of anxiety that some scenes elicit.

• Change the order of the scenes in your hierarchy. Remember, the hierarchy is like a staircase with evenly measured steps. You are the expert. Only you know how you are responding emotionally.

Identify themes that repeat themselves within your hierarchy. Are there a lot of scenes where the nervousness is related to pleasing other people? Or to a fear of failure? Or a fear of success? Are you overly concerned about how your teacher views you? Once you identify a theme that runs throughout your hierarchy, look around in other areas of your life and see if the same theme is present. The odds are good that it will be, somewhere. By working on your test-taking anxiety, you are also working on making the rest of your life more serene.

Apply these skills to daily life. Over time, as you practice the Systematic Desensitization exercises you will become more aware of when your body feels tension and fear. As you develop this ability, apply it to the rest of your life. Notice when daily tension arises and use that feeling as a cue to relax. Practice Abdominal Breathing, the shortened form of relaxation, or visualize your peaceful scene—whatever method works best for you. In this way you will learn how to relax in the face of reality.

Congratulate yourself often. Even when it seems that progress is slow, facing your fear is an extremely courageous act, and your willingness to enter on this path deserves the utmost commendation.

Taping Systematic Desensitization Sessions

There are, as you know by now, many steps to the Systematic Desensitization process. You may find that you have difficulty remembering which step goes where, or you may tend to forget what step you are actually working on. If keeping track of things isn't your strong suit, record the entire process and play the tape as you practice the techniques. For some people, making a tape turns a confusing muddle of instructions into a sensible sequence of exercises that enables them to overcome their phobia.

Here's how to put a Systematic Desensitization session on tape:

1. Record ten minutes of deep relaxation instructions as outlined in chapter 2. Use the Progressive Muscle Relaxation method, or any other technique that enables you to become relaxed. Give yourself ample time for this. Make sure you leave enough blank space between verbal instructions so that you will have time to experience the process and deepen the relaxation.

2. When you notice that you feel relaxed, let your mind drift into your peaceful scene. Again, use the instructions as outlined in chapter 2. You may want to say something like this:

> *As you feel relaxation stream throughout your body, let your mind wander to your pleasant, relaxing scene. Imagine it in as much detail as you can, as though you were really there. Notice the landscape around you. See all the colors as they sparkle in the sunlight. Feel the warmth of the sun as it envelops your body. And feel the various qualities of the ground underneath you. Take a deep breath, and as you inhale, notice how the air smells. Notice any sounds that are present—of birds, or the leaves rustling, or waves washing over the shore. With each sound you notice, your body becomes more and more relaxed. You are completely at ease in this beautiful, tranquil place . . .*

3. After you have relaxed in your peaceful scene, record the instructions for Systematic Desensitization as outlined below:

> *Imagine yourself in the first scene of your anxiety hierarchy. Look around and visualize everything as vividly as you can. Notice all the details.*

(Pause sixty seconds)

> *As you do this, notice any physical sensations that have become present in your body. Take a moment and completely attend to each sensation.*

(Pause twenty seconds)

> *As you notice any anxiety that you feel, let your coping thought gently enter your awareness. Repeat it over and over as you imagine yourself confident and relaxed, able to deal with whatever comes up. Take a deep breath and as you exhale, say to yourself, "Relax. Let it go. Let all the tension go."*

(Pause twenty seconds)

> *Now, let your mind drift from this scene and enter that tranquil, peaceful place you were in only moments ago. Again, notice the shapes, the sounds, the colors, the smells. Recreate each detail. Feel the relaxation re-enter your body. Put your recorder on pause and stay here until you feel completely relaxed.*

(Pause as long as you need)

If visualizing any scene in your hierarchy brings up any feelings of anxiety, go over this scene again. Take as much time as you need to make it vivid. Notice any feelings of anxiety that may enter your body as you imagine this scene. Then, repeat your coping thought as you imagine yourself handling the situation confidently. Put your recorder on pause for as long as you need to do this.

(Pause as long as you need)

If you entered this last scene still feeling some anxiety, repeat the scene again. If no anxiety was present, move on to the next scene. Look around and visualize everything as vividly as you can. Notice all the details.

(Pause twenty seconds)

(Here, continue to re-record the above instructions starting with "As you do this, notice any physical sensations that have become present in your body ...")

When you have finished, you will have a tape that consists of three parts:

1. Ten minutes of relaxation exercises

2. Two minutes of creating your peaceful scene

3. Instructions for the Systematic Desensitization process (these instructions are repeated so that the tape spans two scenes of your hierarchy)

If you're feeling anxiety as you imagine the scenes, one or two scenes a day is a good rate of progress. Remember, it is important to repeat each scene in your hierarchy until you feel no anxiety while imagining it. Start each day's session with the last scene you were desensitized to on the previous day. You'll probably be able to imagine it without feeling any anxiety. However, if anxiety is present, repeat this scene until all the anxiety dissolves.

5

Seeing Is Believing

In 1971, Joseph Cautela found that you can learn to respond to situations in a different way by first imagining a person performing that behavior exactly as you would like to do it yourself. *Behavior Visualization,* also called Covert Modeling or mentally rehearsing, can help you change any problem behavior for any reason. Productivity, promptness, procrastination, shyness, and problem solving are all behaviors that you can improve by using this technique. Studies have shown that Behavior Visualization, particularly when coupled with good study skills, is an extremely effective way to alleviate test-taking anxiety and improve other academic problem areas.

Here are the three basic steps to practicing Behavior Visualization:

1. Identify which parts of a situation you want to change. (If your problem is test-taking anxiety, you especially want to change the things you do that raise your anxiety level.)

2. Establish the ways in which you would prefer to behave. (These are the behaviors that would help your anxiety level to remain low, or even drop.)

3. Learn this more preferable way of behaving by visualizing others and yourself successfully doing this action over and over again.

Behavior Visualization works best if you imagine a variety of people, including yourself, performing the behavior that you want to change. For example, say the thought of walking into an auditorium where a test is about to be given makes your heart flutter and your knees feel like jelly. Once you have identified this specific scene as one that arouses feelings of anxiety, you can then imagine what other people would do and feel as they performed the same act. Your uncle Harold, the Sumo wrestler, would enter that auditorium in a different way, with a set of feelings different from the ones you would have. Your classmate, who finds test taking a breeze, would sit down in her seat on the day of the test in a different manner, with a different emotional make-up than you would. As you visualize these models performing this specific task, you'll be able to see how each one would react to the events in this scene that cause you distress. You can then imagine yourself living the same scene, employing some of the same mannerisms, coping techniques, and confidence that your imaginary models exhibited.

Instructions for Behavior Visualization

Since the objective of mentally rehearsing your behavior is to change a specific act or action, you need to make sure that your goal is stated in terms of behavioral change, not in terms of emotional change. It's true that your main concern may be to lessen your anxiety level so you can get better grades when you take tests, but the emotions of "feeling less afraid" or "feeling more calm in the lecture hall" are both too vague to mentally rehearse. Instead you first need to figure out what specific things you're doing that correspond to your feelings of anxiety and what specific thoughts you have when you do these things. Do you start to feel anxious when you open your books to study? Do you begin to feel nervous as you walk into the classroom? Does sitting in a library make you break out in a cold sweat? Does your voice break when you try to answer a question out loud in class? Whenever you feel anxiety, that feeling is often linked to either something you're doing, or something you're avoiding doing. The first task in Behavior Visualization is to figure out exactly what these behaviors are.

Step One: Identify the Behavior You Want to Change

Write a paragraph describing the behavior you want to change. Include in your description the specific ways in which you would like to change this behavior. Meet Bill. Here is his description:

> I am a forty-year-old college student who panics every time
> I have to take a test. Regardless of how well I think I know
> the material, when I get the actual test in my hand, I feel my
> mind start to go blank, and my heart start to beat very

quickly. I try to focus on the questions, but I keep thinking that I can't pass this test and that I'll fail the entire class.

All my concentration suddenly goes to figuring out what story I can tell the instructor that will get me out of this situation. I never actually leave the test room, but my performance on the test is low and doesn't reflect my knowledge of the material. I end up answering most of the questions using a fraction of my concentration and needing far more than the allotted time. I'd like to change this behavior and figure out how I can control my seemingly out-of-control emotions.

Next, make a list, breaking down your problem behavior into a sequence of separate steps. To help you think of what these steps might be, you may want to close your eyes and remember the last time you acted in this particular way. Include any recurring thoughts you had in this situation that increased your level of anxiety. Remember to note the changes in your anxiety level as they occurred and the related action or nonaction you were performing when you became anxious. Here are the specific steps for Bill's problem:

1. *I get to the lecture hall twenty minutes before the exam begins because I want to have plenty of time to mentally prepare myself.*

2. *Hoping to find someone else equally as nervous, I ask other students if they feel ready for the test.*

3. *Each time someone mentions an area they don't think they studied well enough, I find myself thinking that I'm going to fail, and my anxiety level mounts.*

4. *I pull out my notes and start looking them over. Suddenly, it seems like I can't remember anything. Frantically, I try to memorize more information.*

5. *When the doors are unlocked to the lecture hall, I sit in the first seat I come to and continue to try to memorize my notes.*

6. *I rifle through my notes until the last minute. As I'm putting them away and getting out my pencil and paper, the instructor is going through the test instructions. I don't hear a word he says.*

7. *When I turn the test over, I realize I haven't heard the instructions and start to panic. My face starts to flush and I feel light-headed.*

8. *I try to scan the questions. Some of them don't seem to make any sense. This adds to my panic. I start thinking that it's all over now. I might as well quit school entirely.*

9. *When I come to the first question I don't know, my anxiety sky-rockets.*

10. *I rescan all the questions to see how many there are that I can't answer. Each one I come across ups my anxiety level.*

11. *I start trying to think of ways I can get out of this situation. Maybe I could tell the instructor that I'm sick and that I have to leave. Or maybe I could just plain faint. My mind goes around and around trying to figure out whether I could actually pull either of these off.*

12. *Finally I tell myself that I need to answer something, and I go to the true/false and multiple choice sections. When I don't know the answer, I take a guess.*

13. *Answering some questions eases my anxiety a little. But when I get to the essay questions, I start to panic again. I tell myself that I won't be able to answer even half of these questions.*

14. *I start with the essay question that seems most familiar and, certain that I don't have enough time left to finish, quickly write down anything I can remember about the subject, whether the question asks for it or not.*

15. *I answer as many essay questions as I can this way. When the time is up, I haven't finished the last question, and I haven't had any time to look over my answers.*

Step Two: Establish Your Desired Behavior

Look over the steps you wrote down for your problem behavior. As you read each one, highlight or underline the parts where you noted a rise in your level of anxiety. These are the key behaviors you need to change in order to raise your level of test-taking proficiency. You may also notice behaviors that you want to change for reasons unrelated to your level of anxiety. If this is the case, highlight these segments also. Here is the previous list of fifteen steps with the appropriate parts underlined:

1. *I get to the lecture hall twenty minutes before the exam begins because I want to have plenty of time to mentally prepare myself.*

2. *Hoping to find someone else equally as nervous, I ask other students if they feel ready for the test.*

3. *Each time someone mentions an area they don't think they studied well enough, I find myself thinking that I'm going to fail, and my anxiety level mounts.*

4. *I pull out my notes and start looking them over. Suddenly, it seems like I can't remember anything. Frantically, I start trying to memorize more information.*

5. When the doors are unlocked to the lecture hall, I sit in the first seat I come to and continue to try to memorize my notes.

6. I rifle through my notes until the last minute. As I'm putting them away and getting out my pencil and paper, the instructor is going through the test instructions. I don't hear a word he says.

7. *When I turn the test over, I realize I haven't heard the instructions and start to panic.* My face starts to flush and I feel light-headed.

8. *I try to scan the questions. Some of them don't seem to make any sense. This adds to my panic.* I start thinking that its all over now. I might as well quit school entirely.

9. *When I come to the first question I don't know, my anxiety sky-rockets.*

10. *I rescan all the questions to see how many there are that I can't answer. Each one I come across ups my anxiety level.*

11. *I start trying to think of ways I can get out of this situation.* Maybe I could tell the instructor that I'm sick and that I have to leave. Or maybe I could just plain faint. My mind goes around and around trying to figure out whether I could actually pull either of these off.

12. Finally I tell myself that I need to answer something, and I go to the true/false and the multiple choice sections. When I don't know the answer, I take a guess.

13. *Answering some questions eases my anxiety a little. But when I get to the essay questions, I start to panic again.* I tell myself that I won't be able to answer even half of these questions.

14. I start with the essay question that seems most familiar and, certain that I don't have enough time left to finish, *quickly write down anything I can remember* about the subject, whether the question asks for it or not.

15. I answer as many essay questions as I can this way. When the time is up, I haven't finished the last question, and I haven't had any time to look over my answers.

When you're ready to write down the ways in which you want your behavior to change, go through the highlighted segments, analyze each one, then write down the specific problem that seems to explain each instance of increased anxiety or ineffective action. Here is a list of Bill's specific problems:

1. *Talking to other students about things they didn't study well enough*

2. *Getting all wrapped up in thinking about how I'll probably fail and believing these thoughts*

3. *Trying to study and memorize facts right before the test*

4. *Not hearing the instructions for the test*

5. *Not being able to make sense of a question when I do an initial quick scan of the test*

6. *Contemplating whether it might be best to give up now*

7. *Coming to a question I really don't know the answer to*

8. *Concentrating on how many questions I don't know the answer to*

9. *Wasting time imagining how I can get out of this situation*

10. *Believing my thoughts about how badly I'm doing*

11. *Answering essay questions*

This is the list of your behaviors that you'll actually want to change in some way. With this in mind, you're ready to make a list of the ways in which you would prefer to behave. Remember to include any thoughts you had that increased your anxiety and how you would like to cope with these thoughts. Feel free to change as many of the original steps from your problem behavior in whatever way you need to. You may want to combine steps, or break one step down into two or more. Here are the steps for Bill's desired behavior:

1. *I'll arrive at the test site five minutes before the test begins. Doing this will give me just enough time to find a seat and get out the materials I'll need. I won't talk to any students about material that could be on the test, and I won't open a single book or look at a single note.*

2. *I'll take a seat up near the front of the room so that I'll be able to hear the instructions clearly.*

3. *In the few minutes of extra time I have before the test I will do deep breathing and focus my concentration on the physical look of the room. When I find myself thinking about how awful I'm going to do, I'll remind myself that this is just a thought I'm thinking because I'm scared.*

4. *As the instructions are read, I will listen carefully and continue with my deep breathing.*

5. *When I get the test, I'll read through all instructions carefully twice. But I won't read the content of any specific questions yet.*

6. *I will answer any true/false, multiple choice, or short answer sections first. Answering some questions will help me feel more confident.*

7. *When I come to an answer I don't know, I'll skip it and come back to it after I finish the other questions. Since this will probably make me feel scared, I'll do a minute of deep breathing and refute any panicky thoughts that I have with coping statements.*

8. *When I get to the essay questions, I'll carefully read each one. Then I'll let thoughts and images about the question form for a couple of minutes as I do deep breathing. I'll feel more confident here than usual because I'll have made a special effort to study potential essay questions before the test. When I am ready to write down the answer, I'll first make a brief outline on scrap paper.*

9. *If at any time I feel as though I'm starting to panic or lose control, I won't waste time trying to think of an excuse to leave. Instead, I'll practice the relaxation exercises that I know work well, use my coping statements, and do deep breathing.*

Step Three: Visualize Your Desired Behavior

Bring the environment to life. Before you begin visualizing the sequential steps of your desired behavior, spend a few minutes imaging the physical room where this behavior will occur. If the behavior you want to change relates to how you take tests, you'll want to visualize the room where the test will be given. Does it have desks, or chairs with tables, or is it an auditorium? What does it feel like to physically sit in these chairs? When you sit in this chair, what are the sounds that you hear? What kind of lighting is there? Are there windows that let sunlight in? Fluorescent lights on the ceiling? Do these lights make a humming noise? Does the instructor stand on a stage? At the front of the room, or in the center? What is the instructor wearing? What does the floor look like? Carpet? Linoleum? Wood? Do the walls have pictures or posters on them? Is there a chalkboard? Does the room have a certain smell? Can you recreate it in your imagination? Bring to mind as many details as you can. Remember to recreate details that you gather from at least three of your senses.

Visualize your models. Imagine someone who is very different from you walking into the test room that you have just visualized.

Although the physical look of this person will differ from your own, the critical difference should be one of attitude. For instance, you could imagine a person who couldn't care less about how he or she performs on a test. Or you could imagine someone who is just dripping with confidence. Or you could view someone who has an important meeting next period and sees the test simply as a nuisance that must be endured until then.

As your model takes the test (or studies for the test, or participates in class, or does any activity that you want to perform differently), imagine that person in detail as he or she encounters all the frustrations and upsets that you would experience in the same situation. Each time your model has a problem, watch carefully as he or she solves it. Notice when your model behaves in a manner that you would like to emulate.

Next, imagine someone with an attitude similar to your own taking the test. Recreate the fear, the dread, the mind that remembers nothing. As you watch this person try to cope with each problem and frustration as it comes up, you'll experience some of the fear you're imagining your model feels. When this happens, see if you can replace any feeling of fear with a feeling of compassion for your model as he or she struggles with the pressure of having to perform while terrified. Then, as you empathetically view your model's trials, imagine fear diminishing, confidence rising, and memory and ability becoming greater. Your model completes the test exuberantly, and as he or she does, you feel the victory as one that you both contributed to equally.

Finally, imagine yourself taking the test. As you come across each pitfall, see yourself cope with your emotions confidently. Then, after you imagine every problem that you can think of, see yourself completing the test successfully with ease and confidence. As you watch yourself finish the test, imagine the sense of pride and elation you feel, knowing as you do the obstacles you had to overcome to reach this accomplishment.

Perform your ideal behavior in real life, then write a short review of how it went. Writing this review will show you how this technique has helped you change your behavior. Here is Bill's review:

> *Before the test I didn't talk to anyone except to say "Hi"*
> *and I didn't look at my notes or books. I sat close to the*
> *front of the class and heard all the instructions. Already,*
> *my anxiety level seemed lower than usual. I answered the*
> *true/false, multiple choice, and short-answer questions first,*
> *then went on to the essay questions. Here, I started to*
> *panic for a minute, but I remembered to breathe deeply*
> *and to tell myself that I was all right and that all I had to*

do was take things one step at a time. Doing this seemed to
help. Out of five essay questions, there was one I didn't
answer very well and one other that I could've answered
better. I ended up getting ten points taken off for one of them
and three for the other. I also missed a couple of short-answer
questions, which was another three points off. I ended up with
a B- on this test. Although I still think I knew the material
better than this grade indicates, I did do much better than I
would have otherwise.

Working on Other Problem Behaviors

You have just seen an example of how changing your behavior during
a test can help you lower your level of anxiety. You can optimize your
ability to do well by changing your behavior during critical times that
lead up to the test. On the next few pages are several examples of how
to change possible problem behaviors into more desirable ones. First,
each problem is defined, then that behavior is divided into sequential
steps. Next, the sequential steps for the desired behavior are listed.
Finally, there is a review of what happened when the actual behavior
was performed in real life.

Sleeping

The Problem

On the night before any test, I go to bed early so I can be well
rested the next day. But I always wake up during the night and can't
get back to sleep. I feel exhausted for the rest of the day, including
when I'm taking the test.

Sequential Steps of Problem Behavior

1. I go to bed at 11 P.M.

2. I wake up around 2 A.M.

3. I close my eyes and try to sleep, but the material for the test
   has already started to run through my brain.

4. I lie in bed and try to remember all the facts I need for tomorrow's test, while realizing that what I really need to do is to
   go back to sleep.

5. By 4 A.M. I've worked myself into a state of panic about not
   getting enough sleep, and I realize that going back to sleep will
   be impossible. I reluctantly get up and make myself some tea.

6. I figure that as long as I'm up, I might as well go through some of the lists I wrote up for the test.

7. Although my mind seems to be racing a hundred miles a minute, my memory is dull and I miss many of the facts that I thought I had down earlier in the evening. This shakes up my confidence even more.

8. By 5 A.M., I haven't made any headway, but my mind's still racing. I sit on the couch and watch old "I Love Lucy" reruns.

9. I drift off to sleep around 6:30. At 7:30 I hear my alarm in the next room go off. I get up.

10. After a shower and coffee I feel only slightly less zombie-like than I did when woke up. At 9 A.M., I arrive in class feeling much less mentally alert than I did in the middle of the night.

Sequential Steps of Desired Behavior

1. I go to bed at midnight instead of 11, thinking that doing this will help me sleep for a longer period than I otherwise would.

2. I wake up at 4:30 A.M. I've already had four-and-a-half hours of sleep. I tell myself that even if I don't go back to sleep, I've already slept enough to be coherent for the test.

3. Although my mind wants to think about the test, every time I notice a thought, I mentally replace it with the image of my peaceful scene.

4. At around 5 A.M., I drift off again and get in another couple of hours of peaceful sleep.

5. My alarm goes off at 7:30 A.M., and I wake up feeling alert.

Reviewing the Actual Behavior

I went to bed at midnight and woke up just after 4 A.M. I remembered that four hours was enough rest, and reminded myself that, even if I didn't go back to sleep, it was no big deal. As I lay in bed, I recreated my peaceful scene in my imagination. Whenever I started to worry about the test, I returned immediately to my peaceful scene. Eventually, I dozed off again for about another hour. I got up around 6 A.M., showered, made coffee, and studied for about an hour. Although I didn't sleep soundly through the entire night, I felt that I did get enough sleep and that I was mentally alert.

Studying

The Problem

Whenever I set aside a block of time to study, I feel like I waste a lot of it and end up not knowing too much more than I did before I began studying.

Sequential Steps of Problem Behavior

1. I sit down to go over my text, but my mind keeps wandering onto other things.

2. After about an hour of slowly progressing through my reading, I decide that I need a cup of coffee to pick me up.

3. I go to the kitchen and make some coffee, then to the living room to continue my reading.

4. My roommate comes home and turns on the TV. I continue reading with part of my mind while keeping track of the TV show with another part.

5. After the program is over, I go back to my room. I realize that I really haven't retained very much of the information I've read and decide the best thing to do is to start taking notes.

6. Although taking notes seems to help me memorize, it slows down my progress through the chapter. And I need to finish up two chapters by this evening.

7. I realize that I'm not going to finish the reading I had planned to finish. I start to feel scared and depressed. I spend some time worrying about my final grade in the class.

8. I reason that maybe my class notes will give me a hint about the information I'll need to know for the test. I pull out my notes and start to thumb through them.

9. I read over a list of important dates and events several times. I'm just at the point where I feel I know it pretty well and it's time to leave for work.

Sequential Steps for Desired Behavior

1. I sit down with my text, a pen, and a notebook. I realize that even though taking notes will add to the time it takes me to study, it will also help me keep my mind on what I'm doing and help me memorize the material. I adjust the time I've estimated I'll need for studying to account for this.

2. As soon as I notice other thoughts enter my mind, I drop them and return my mind to my reading.

3. At the end of every hour of studying, I take a ten-minute break for coffee or whatever. I make sure this break lasts only ten minutes.

4. I only study in a quiet room without distractions.

5. During the last part of my study period, I recite the notes that I've just taken.

6. I go through the notes one more time before bedtime. This will help the information stick in my memory.

Reviewing the Actual Behavior

I started studying for my history class at 3 P.M. Although it was hard to get started, I stuck with it and eventually reached a point where I felt involved with the material. I took notes on this reading as I had planned to and this did seem to increase my ability to remember things. I took a break every hour or so, but it was hard to limit it to just ten minutes, and several times it ran over. Although I didn't have too much time for this, I did briefly review the notes I took before I left for work. I looked at them once again before bedtime. I ended up feeling much better than I usually do about this study session.

Asking a Question in Class

The Problem

Sometimes the instructor makes a statement during class that I don't understand. I want to ask for clarification, but I am afraid that the rest of the class will think the question is silly. Consequently, I never raise my hand.

Sequential Steps of Problem Behavior

1. I'm taking notes in class.

2. The instructor makes a statement.

3. I realize that I'm confused about this statement.

4. I formulate a question in my mind.

5. I decide to wait and see if someone else will ask the question.

6. No one asks. The instructor moves on to the next topic. I decide to wait and ask my question after class.

7. About six other students are waiting to talk to the instructor after class. I am the last one.

8. I try to overhear the questions that the others are asking, hoping that someone will ask my question.

9. As I continue to wait, I decide that my question really isn't that important—that I'll probably be able to figure it out myself at home.

10. I leave the class.

Sequential Steps for Desired Behavior

1. I'm taking notes in class.

2. The instructor makes a statement.

3. I realize I'm confused about this statement.

4. I formulate a question in my mind.

5. Without considering what others may think, I raise my hand.

6. The instructor calls my name.

7. Even though I'm afraid that I'll make a mistake, I open my mouth and begin speaking.

8. I finish asking the entire question. No one laughs or thinks I am silly.

9. The instructor answers my question and I take down notes.

10. I feel a sense of pride for having accomplished a task that I felt so anxious about doing.

Reviewing the Actual Behavior

I was taking notes in class when I noticed I wasn't clear about what the instructor was saying. I took a moment to think about my question, and then I raised my hand. When the instructor called my name, I felt a wave of terror go through my chest, and I was certain my voice would shake when I asked the question. But I got it all out, and no one else seemed to notice. As the instructor explained the point, I took notes—I was still so nervous I knew that I wouldn't be able to remember. But, I did feel good about speaking in class, even though I was terrified.

6

So Many Excuses,
So Little Time

Almost everyone who suffers from test-taking anxiety has developed the practice of procrastination into a fine art. One reading assignment slides into and merges with the next assignment. Reviewing notes and reciting facts are put off until a few days before the test. Cramming sessions are much less fruitful than originally imagined. So, when the actual test rolls around, often the procrastination experts become inflicted with either real or imaginary ailments and are then forced to take an incomplete for that class until this work is made up. Months pass, and with a new semester's worth of work looming on the horizon, last semester's incomplete sinks slowly toward the land where all the little incompletes grow into big, fat Fs.

What Is Procrastination?

You procrastinate when you have clearly decided upon a goal, and you postpone doing the thing (or things) you need to do in order to obtain that goal. In other words, after you realize what it is that you want, you deliberately put off doing whatever you need to do to get it.

Usually, procrastination is not simply a matter of managing your time poorly. Like all anxiety-driven behaviors, it is a complex combination of thoughts, feelings, and actions (or in this case, inaction). Each of these components directly interacts with each of the others until you have a big ball of resistance built up between you and the thing you want to accomplish. You do all this in an attempt to avoid feeling the anxiety that's woven throughout your life.

The thoughts and feelings involved in procrastination usually operate in a cyclical pattern. The thought of approaching or doing a task initially makes you feel anxious, or antsy, or afraid, or angry for any one of many possible reasons. You then think, possibly unconsciously, that putting off doing this task will let you avoid the accompanying anxiety for just a little longer. It's almost as if you believe that by avoiding this anxious feeling now, it will just disappear entirely. But whenever you do actually get around to approaching the task, that jumpy, antsy, uncomfortable feeling is still there, still waiting for you to feel it.

You continue to put off doing the task until a shift in feeling occurs. That shift happens when, as the deadline quickly approaches, the fear you have of not getting the task done becomes larger than the fear you have of actually doing the task. At this point, fear is running a large part of your life. Whether you are avoiding or beginning the task, fear is your motivation.

To see how all the parts of procrastination might fit together, let's look at Tim, whose history final is coming up at the end of the week. Participating in activities in which someone will judge his performance has always been a problem for Tim, and taking tests is the activity that makes him the most nervous. Whenever he sits down with his books to begin studying, he notices that his heart starts to beat a little faster, and his breathing starts to get a little shallow. As he opens his history text to the first page, his attention is pulled from the material he is reading to self-absorbed, worried thoughts. "There is too much to remember," he thinks. "How will I ever be able to figure out what questions will actually be on the test? I wish I had paid better attention in class."

As each of these thoughts pops up, Tim feels more and more nervous. He reads a whole page of text, and then realizes that he wasn't paying attention while he was doing this reading. Most of his attention was wrapped up in his worried thoughts, and he didn't really know what the reading was about. As he realizes this, his heart races a little faster, and his breath gets a little more shallow. He feels much less comfortable than he did before he started studying. He begins the second page, but has to read the first paragraph four times before he actually gets what it says. "At this rate, I'll be studying forever. Maybe I'll just wait until tomorrow when I can concentrate better."

But the next day Tim's concentration isn't any better. Nor is it the next day, or the day after that. Finally on Thursday, four days before the test, Tim realizes that his concentration might not get any better, at least not in time to study for this test. He resolves to sit down and study regardless of how well he is able to stay focused. Having mentally made this commitment, Tim's concentration surprisingly gets much sharper. He is able to cover the material more quickly. However, by now he has lost three days of valuable time and ends up doing less well on the test than he knew he could have if he'd studied during those first three days.

Why People Procrastinate

Although there are many reasons for and ways of procrastinating, behind most instances of procrastination there is a single, basic premise that reads something like this:

> I don't want to do this. But, if I don't do it, something
> will happen that I don't want to have happen. Therefore,
> I will do this thing, but not because I choose to. Someone
> is making me do it.

A variety of emotions can emerge from this pressure to perform or act. You can feel the fear of leaving your comfort zone of daily activity. You might feel victimized, or resentful, or rebellious because you are "being forced" to do this thing. You could feel angry at feeling pushed around or anxious to do your best. This situation of having to do something that you don't want to do can bring up a whole host of feelings that may lead you to become stressed, confused, or depressed. And so, in order to avoid this hornets' nest of emotion, you put off the task—for just a little bit longer. Surely a little bit couldn't hurt that much . . .

The Faces of Fear

Although the basis of procrastination is anxiety, this anxiety can take on any number of different forms. For instance, it could feel like boredom, or restlessness, or anger, or simply the angst of wanting to be doing something else. Whatever the negative emotion is, its root is usually one of fear, and it causes you to divert your effort so that you avoid the task you need to complete in favor of doing something less uncomfortable.

Which face your anxiety wears depends on your inner belief system that evolved as you were growing up and that now includes one or more mistaken beliefs. (For more on this, see "Where Self-Talk Comes From" in chapter 3.) These are ideas that you developed when you were younger about yourself, others, or the way the world operates that are wrong, or at least are wrong much of the time. By now, these ideas are so integral to the way you see reality that it seldom occurs to you that they are simply something that you believe. Some examples of mistaken beliefs might be: "It's bad to be angry," "If I take a chance,

I'll fail," "If I don't do well I'm worthless," or "If I worry long enough, I can ward off any danger."

Often, mistaken beliefs express an underlying fear. For example, "If I take a chance, I'll fail" is really a fear of failure. Or, "If I don't do well, I'm worthless" is really a fear of not being liked because you're imperfect.

Below is a list of some of the mistaken beliefs that can lead to chronic procrastination. In the first four mistaken beliefs, procrastination is a way to maintain your perceived sense of worth, thereby lessening the threat of rejection.

- **Fear of failure.** The belief that if you try to accomplish something and then fail, this decreases your basic value as a person.

- **Fear of criticism.** The belief that when someone you respect tells you you're wrong, this lessens your value as a human being.

- **Fear of rejection.** The belief that if you don't do well at a task, people won't like you; this takes away from your essential worth.

- **Fear of being overwhelmed.** The belief that if you try anything that you're very anxious or nervous about, you then won't be able to complete the task.

- **Fear of commitment.** The belief that if you succeed at completing a task, this will some how lock you into a group of activities, or trap you into a way of being that you won't like. Procrastinating is a way of delaying until your path becomes clearer or more compelling so that you will avoid making a mistake.

- **Fear of boredom or restlessness.** The belief that if your interest isn't stimulated at all times, you will feel terrible. Here, you procrastinate by sinking yourself into pleasurable activities in order to avoid your anxiety.

- **Fear of the angst of wanting.** The belief that if you deny yourself something that you really want to do, you will feel terrible. (This is similar to the fear of boredom, but with more emotion attached.)

- **Fear of powerlessness.** The belief that if someone else has total power over an aspect of your life (as teachers do), he or she will then hurt you in some way. Procrastinating, in this case, is a way of trying to even out the balance of power. ("I have some control over when I hand this paper in. It isn't entirely yours.") In this case, the feeling of anger often masks the fear.

- **Fear of success.** The belief that if you really know what you want, and try to achieve something and succeed, then everyone will know who you really are. Procrastinating is a way of continuing to hide.

But It Feels So Rewarding

In all of the preceding cases, procrastinating is a way to avoid doing a task or activity (in this case reading, writing, and studying) that would bring up feelings of anxiety, nervousness, and even anger. Since you initially feel better when you avoid the task, procrastinating seems, at first, like a good choice. You recreate the initial sense of relief that procrastination brings about by learning to repeat this behavior over and over again. Procrastinating then becomes a firmly entrenched habit. You forget that your anxiety or nervousness will eventually skyrocket beyond the level you originally felt. It's this amped up anxiety that either motivates you to complete the task or causes you to bail out entirely.

Finding Reasons to Procrastinate

Although the main reason you procrastinate is to avoid the unpleasant sensations that doing the task brings up, you usually tell yourself that whatever is going on is something completely different. Here are some of the more common excuses used to postpone working on a project:

"I don't feel like it right now." Often, the illusion that if you just wait long enough, something similar to inspiration or a kind of "readiness" will envelop you and heighten your senses of brilliance and creativity. Although this may be true for some people or for some projects, for most, inspiration comes about after they actually sit down and engage their thoughts with whatever they're working on for a while. Focusing your attention on a task often has a beneficial side effect of calling up your creative self.

"Other things seem so compelling." Sometimes people grow up in an environment that doesn't positively reinforce their ability to know who they are and what they want. Consequently, many people learn to lose themselves in mountains of minutiae, and never learn to differentiate between that which is important and that which is trivial. These people are always very busy. But as soon as they sit down to complete a term paper that's due tomorrow, they suddenly feel a pressing need to clean out the cupboard that they've been meaning to get to for weeks. To approach the attainment of a personal goal seems dangerous, and it feels safer to space out on any personal wishes.

"If only _____ was different, I could do it. It's not really my fault." Sometimes people assume that one small part of their lives is so critical that it governs the outcome of many of their endeavors. In school, this importance is often assigned to the instructor, manifesting itself in thoughts such as, "If only he graded more fairly I'd be able to do better. Why even bother?" or "If only she liked me more, she'd explain things better to me." It's easier to give up if it seems that someone else is responsible for the problem. One way to test for these blaming thoughts is to see whether the words "If only" can be inserted at the beginning of the thought. When you identify blaming thoughts, focus on how the responsibility is really yours and on what *you* can do to accomplish the task.

"I feel too emotional. I can't deal with studying now." Often emotions seem so strong or uncomfortable that you focus all your attention on the situation or event that brought up the emotion. If someone you like cancels a date for what seems like a not too important reason, or if your hours are cut back at work, the emotions brought up by these events may seem overwhelming. However, there can be a fine line between emotional recuperation and procrastination. Learning how to tolerate the physical sensations of strong emotions and how to calm yourself when they arise are two valuable techniques that will help you "get over it and get on with it" sooner. (See chapter 2.)

"I can't do this perfectly. I might as well not even try." Perfectionists, at some point in their lives, have confused the completed product with their inner sense of worth. Anything less than perfection is seen as a failure. And this failure, so they reason, will then invite rejection, mockery, or ridicule from others. The fear of this imagined intense scrutiny often stops perfectionists in their tracks. Instead of facing the criticism that failure will most certainly bring, they often convince themselves that it's better to not try at all. Then, as the deadline approaches, their fear escalates, and eventually they begin the task. However, by this point there is little time left, and the perfectionist is unable to get the work done as "perfectly" as possible. This, then, may serve as an excuse—"if only there was more time, I could have done it better. But since there wasn't, this is passable." So, in a sense, perfectionists' procrastination can be a way of giving themselves permission to try at all without the stressful thought that only perfection will do.

"I don't have the materials I need." When you're looking for a way to justify putting off work on a project, often you sabotage yourself by not getting everything you need together before you start. Suddenly, when you finally do sit down to work, you realize that you don't have the one book you really need, and the library doesn't have it, and the

bookstores are closed. You can't imagine how you could possibly go forward with your task without this one item. You can't see any option other than to work on the project at another time.

I don't have to do this now. It isn't really that important. Sometimes, rather than face the anxiety of completing a task, you instead choose to imagine that your goals are somehow different than they really are. Let's say you started the semester with the intention of finishing up the classes you need to get a B.A. You may find yourself thinking, as your work mounts up and the semester speeds along, that getting your B.A. at the end of this semester isn't really that important. After all, you could go back to school next semester. What's the hurry, anyway? You have all the time in the world, right? This kind of thinking can cause you to veer off the track that leads to where you want to go and end up at a different, often entirely unsatisfying destination.

"I have too many other things that need to be done." It's true that most people are living very busy, demanding lives these days. In addition to their studies, many students have responsibilities to their families and their jobs. However, even when you know how to find the time, you often use these responsibilities as an excuse for postponing studying or writing term papers. Be aware of which tasks are truly necessary and which, if any, are ones you use to provide yourself with a convenient out.

"This won't take very long. I don't have to start it now." Sometimes, in an attempt to avoid anxious feelings, people lull themselves into a sense of security by thinking that they have plenty of time and can always do it later. This is seldom the case with studying. The nature of learning and memorizing demands that little pieces of schoolwork be done frequently over a long spread of time. And, if this false rationale is applied to every class, clearly the amount of work that will accumulate towards the end of the term will be unmanageable.

Are You a Chronic Procrastinator?

Most chronic procrastinators share some of the seven following characteristics:

1. You always feel that there is something else that has to be done *now*. Often, it is something that suddenly seems more pressing, but objectively is much less important, than the task you are avoiding.

2. You are unwilling to come to grips with a realistic concept of time. To a procrastinator, things will always take much less

time than they actually do. And, there always seems to be more time in which to do them than there actually is.

3. You are generally vague about personal values and goals. Specifics are often ignored. By keeping your goal undefined, it seems easier to change it, or let go of it entirely, if it appears that you won't achieve it.

4. You lack the confidence that, if you do put forth your best effort, you will actually be able to reach your goal.

5. You mistakenly believe that if your goal is obtained, you will be less safe than you were before you reached your goal.

6. You often confuse self-worth with the task that needs to be accomplished. This confusion is often expressed by the illogical fear of making a mistake.

7. You have a persistent or nagging sense of frustration. Habitual procrastinators will often describe themselves as unfulfilled, or not living up to their potential.

Understanding the problem is only part of the battle to conquer procrastination. You also need to know which techniques will help, and—the most important part—you need to actually follow them. To combat procrastination, you will need to follow three basic steps:

1. Set realistic, specific, and measurable goals.

2. Schedule or plan your life in a way that will allow you to achieve your goals.

3. Take action; follow your plan.

Setting Goals

Setting up the goals in your life is like opening up a set of Russian nesting dolls—for every goal you think of, there is one or more smaller goals right inside of it. For example, let's say your goal is to become a social worker. Before you can do that, you have to go back to college and get a degree. Before you get your degree, you have to pass a certain number of specific classes. But in order to pass these classes, you need to successfully pass tests and write papers for each of these classes. And in order to pass tests, you need to read and study a certain amount of material each week. Each one of these steps can be seen as a goal. Your long-term goal is to become a social worker. Your short-term goal is to spend thirty to forty hours a week reading, studying, and attending classes. You can break this down even further by establishing what goals you want to accomplish in each twenty-four-hour period, and even exactly when you want to have them done by.

Since this book is about test-taking anxiety, the goals it focuses on are mostly of an academic nature. However, it is important to also establish and work on goals in the other areas of your life. Your family and friends, your health, your recreational activities, your financial assets, and your spiritual development are all areas in which you can evaluate what you want, and how you would like to approach it. Keeping a balance between the opposites—work and play, solitude and camaraderie, physical exertion and rest, family time and study time, and so on, is one way to experience the satisfaction of a meaningful and fulfilling life.

Be Specific

The goals you set will be most helpful if they are specific. Your mind can lose track of a vaguely stated goal. If you say your goal is to learn to play the piano, and then you do nothing for the next two months, your mind can still think that you're in the process of working your way up to maybe thinking about looking for a piano instructor and a piano to practice on. However, stating that your goal is to get a piano within two weeks, find a teacher and start piano lessons by the beginning of next month, and practice for an hour six days a week gives your mind a way of assessing whether your goal is being met or not.

Make Your Goal Observable and Measurable

Your goal will be of little value if there is no way to gauge whether you've made progress toward it or not. Bearing this in mind, it is important to define goals in terms of behavior, not feelings. If you said something like, "My goal is to feel less nervous," you have not given yourself any guidelines illustrating specifically how you will actually obtain that goal. The goal here is not a behavior that can be watched, but a feeling, which is subjective. How will you know when your feeling of nervousness is less or more than it used to be? And if it's less, what made it less? And even if it's less, is it enough less? And is feeling less nervous something you are constantly moving toward, or is it something that just happens every now and then?

However, the goal of "feeling less nervous" can easily be defined in terms of behavior. First, you would need to define what you mean by "less nervous." Do you mean that you want to do things that you now avoid because doing them causes you to feel nervous? Do you mean you want to reduce the overall level of anxiety in your life from maybe a ten to a five? Or do you mean that when you feel nervous you would like to be able to calm your body down or slow down your thoughts? Once you've decided what "less nervous" means to you, you can then write down short-term behavioral goals that, if met, will lead you to feel "less nervous." For instance, if you meant that you wanted to learn to calm yourself down once you became nervous, you could state a goal like this: "I'm going to practice Progressive Muscle Relaxation for twenty minutes, twice every day." Since this is an action, it is easy to tell whether you have completed it or not.

Goals should also be measurable. You can measure your goals in one of two ways: the amount of time you spend working towards your goal, or the number of things that are actually accomplished. If you choose to measure your goal in terms of time you spend on it, you'll use phrases such as "an hour every day," "ten hours a week," "two days a month," or "three times every other week." If you choose to measure your goal in terms of what you accomplish, you'll make statements like "read fifty pages a day," "write five pages every day," or "read a book over the weekend." In general, it's better to measure your goals in terms of the time you spend on them. Procrastinators are particularly good at being unrealistic about how long a task will actually take. Reading a book over the weekend may, in reality, be an impossible task.

Divide Your Goal into Observable Steps

Once you have developed a clear idea of what it is that you want to accomplish, figure out the specific steps you need to take by working backwards from the finished goal. For instance, let's say your goal is to write and turn in a term paper in three weeks. Starting backwards, *the steps leading to your paper's completion could look like this:*

1. *Turn in my term paper on time—May 4.*

2. *Review and incorporate suggestions of two of my classmates who have read my paper at my request—May 1 to May 3.*

3. *Give copies of my paper to two of my classmates to critique—April 29.*

4. *Make copies of my paper—April 29.*

5. *Write a final draft—April 27 to 29.*

6. *Write first draft—April 21 to 27.*

7. *Make an outline of my paper—April 19 to 21.*

8. *Go to library and do research for paper—April 14 to 19.*

9. *Write down initial ideas, concepts, and themes for paper—April 13.*

You will probably find that you need to adjust the deadlines as you progress through each step. However, writing a list of steps and deadlines will keep you aware of the passage of time—how much time has elapsed, how much time you may need for further steps, and how much work you need to do in the time you have left.

Decide Why You Want to Achieve Your Goal

List ten reasons why you want to achieve this goal (even if you don't think there really are ten). For instance, ten reasons to complete the term paper you're writing on time could be:

1. *I need to do this so I can pass this class and then reach my ultimate goal of becoming a social worker.*

2. *If I don't become a social worker, I could end up working at something I really don't like just to make money.*

3. *If I don't become a social worker, I won't be able to help people in the same way.*

4. *Writing this paper can teach me how to deal with the panic I feel about keeping to a deadline.*

5. *I'll learn a lot about (the subject).*

6. *I'll get to flirt with the cute librarian.*

7. *If I hand this paper in on time, I'll stay in the good graces of the instructor.*

8. *I'll learn how to deal with things that distract my attention.*

9. *If I don't hand this paper in on time, I'll feel like I failed.*

10. *If I don't hand this paper in on time and I get an incomplete, the time I'll spend on finishing the paper is really time I'll need to study for the final.*

After you have written down all your reasons, arrange them in order from most important to least important, then make several copies of this list. Put one where it is clearly noticeable in your study area. Post the others in areas where you will likely spend your time instead of studying. If you tend to space out in front of the TV, put one on top of the TV. If you spend time driving around with your friends instead of studying, put one up inside the door of your car. You want these reminders posted in the places where your mind is likely to wander off onto other things.

Notice That You Are Choosing to Study

Every time you sit down to study, read the list of reasons you want to complete this task. Weigh the pros and the cons and then notice that you are making the conscious choice to study. It is not really something that is being forced upon you.

Making Your Plan

Many people have a strange, somewhat hazy sense of time. To them, time seems like an ethereal substance that drifts throughout the activities in their lives. We hear these people say things like, "I don't know where all the time goes," or "I'll do it if there's enough time," as though this substance called "time" might be there, or might have been blown off to somewhere else.

Instead, time is really more like a container that holds your life. Like any container, it can only hold a certain amount of substance, in this case activities, before it fills up completely. But, sometimes there is more life—more that you want to do—than will fit in your container. It's at this point when you have to do some rearranging. Some things will have to be tossed out of the container so that others can be put into it. But you don't want to throw out the things that are important to you. Instead, it makes more sense to toss the things that have less use, or less value, or that you simply don't like as much as the others.

Making a successful antiprocrastination time management plan involves:

1. Evaluating which activities are valuable to you, and which aren't

2. Replacing an adequate number of activities that are low on your value scale with the thing that you're trying to accomplish

3. Keeping a schedule so that you can monitor your progress and meet your deadlines

Finding the Time: Keeping a Daily Log

Most people have little idea about what they actually do with a large portion of their time. They know what they do with the larger chunks: the time at work, the time at class, or the time spent training for the marathon. But the things that take less time, or are of less importance, often get lost. Did you watch television for an hour or two hours? Did you play softball for two hours or three hours? Did your coffee break actually last for ten minutes, or was it forty? And if you pick the kids up, buy groceries, and cook dinner, will there really still be time to read a chapter in your biology text?

In order to be in control of your time, you first have to know how you are spending it now. The following exercise is designed to help you do just that.

The Daily Log

Keep a daily log of all your activities for one week Every half hour or so pull out your log sheet and write down exactly what you have been doing for the past half hour. At the end of the week, you will know approximately how much of your time you spend sleeping, working, eating, talking on the phone, shopping, commuting, watching TV, or taking care of the kids. Once you know how you spend your time, you will be able to figure out which of your activities hold the least value for you. You can then either cut down the time you spend on them, or cut them out of your life altogether.

Estimating Time: The Two-Column Daily Log

Procrastinators often tend to be wishful thinkers about how much time tasks and activities will actually require. It always seems like there will be more time than there actually is. And it always seems like things can be done more quickly than they really can. In order to manage your time more effectively, you need to be able to accurately gauge two things:

1. The amount of time your work will actually take

2. The amount of time you actually have to complete a given task

You can practice estimating the amount of time that tasks require by using a two-column daily log. In the first column, before you begin a task, estimate the amount of time that you think it will take. After you complete the task, write down the amount of time the task actually took in the second column. Make estimates for three days, then evaluate your daily logs. Notice when the amount of projected time to do a task was vastly different than the actual amount of time that it took. Then complete the following statements (you can repeat the third and forth statement as many times as you need to):

1. I want to have more time in my life to _____
   _____ .

2. When I examined my daily logs, I was surprised that _____
   _____ .

3. I want to spend less time doing _____
   _____ .

Daily Log

Time	Activity
7:00 7:30	
8:00 8:30	
9:00 9:30	
10:00 10:30	
11:00 11:30	
Noon 12:30	
1:00 1:30	
2:00 2:30	
3:00 3:30	
4:00 4:30	
5:00 5:30	
6:00 6:30	
7:00 7:30	
8:00 8:30	
9:00 9:30	
10:00 10:30	
11:00 11:30	
Midnight 12:30	
1:00 1:30	
2:00 2:30	

Sample Daily Log

Time	Activity
7:00 7:30	*shower and* *breakfast*
8:00 8:30	*commute to school* *prepare for class*
9:00 9:30	*class*
10:00 10:30	
11:00 11:30	*read for class*
Noon 12:30	*lunch*
1:00 1:30	*prepare for class* *class*
2:00 2:30	
3:00 3:30	*commute home* *change*
4:00 4:30	*jog*
5:00 5:30	*watch* *news*
6:00 6:30	*dinner*
7:00 7:30	*study*
8:00 8:30	
9:00 9:30	*dishes*
10:00 10:30	*laundry*
11:00 11:30	*relax*
Midnight 12:30	*sleep*
1:00 1:30	
2:00 2:30	

4. Instead of spending _____ (amount of time) on
_____ (item), I want to cut it down to _____ (time).

5. This will free up an additional _____
(minutes or hours) in my day that I can use to do something
that is more important to me.

Scheduling Your Time

People often cringe at the thought of scheduling every activity of
their week and then actually sticking to that schedule. They instantly
feel shackled, stifled, and chained to the clock. When these feelings
come up, the weekly schedule can suddenly seem like a cruel task
master that must be fought against in order to maintain a sense of
personal dignity. In reality, making out a weekly schedule is the only
way your mind's eye can actually see a map of your currently uncom-
mitted time that is available to use for studying. It lets you see the
maximum amount of time that you could possibly use to accomplish
a certain project. And, if done right, sticking to a schedule need not
be the grueling chore it may at first seem.

In his book *The Now Habit* (1989), psychologist Neil Fiore presents
a method of scheduling (or "un-scheduling," as he calls it) your time
that is designed specifically for procrastinators. Instead of marking the
blocks of time you will use to sit down and study, you instead record
on your schedule blocks of thirty-minute periods that you have already
used for studying *after you have actually done it.* This means that instead
of recording what you should be doing (but probably aren't), you are
accumulating visual proof of what you have already successfully accomplished. Suddenly, you may find yourself hitting the books more
often because you're looking forward to stacking up more little units
of success. And, although studying may not become exactly enthralling,
it will start to have a rewarding side that you may find compelling.

Here are some benefits of keeping a schedule:

- By aiming at thirty-minute study periods, your task will seem
  much more manageable, and therefore less frightening and
  overwhelming.

- Since the task doesn't seem overwhelming, you are more likely
  to actually sit down and work on your assignment.

- Keeping track of thirty-minute slices of accomplished work will
  motivate you to study more often. You will feel rewarded immediately and often.

- The "un-schedule" schedules in committed blocks of time for
  fun, socializing, recreation, and other forms of play. This assures

Two-column Daily Log

Time	Estimated	Required
7:00 7:30		
8:00 8:30		
9:00 9:30		
10:00 10:30		
11:00 11:30		
Noon 12:30		
1:00 1:30		
2:00 2:30		
3:00 3:30		
4:00 4:30		
5:00 5:30		
6:00 6:30		
7:00 7:30		
8:00 8:30		
9:00 9:30		
10:00 10:30		
11:00 11:30		
Midnight 12:30		
1:00 1:30		
2:00 2:30		

Sample Two-column Daily Log

Time	Estimated	Required
7:00 7:30	*shower and* *breakfast*	*shower and* *breakfast*
8:00 8:30	*commute to school* *prepare for class*	*commute to school*
9:00 9:30	*class*	*class*
10:00 10:30	↓	↓
11:00 11:30	*lunch*	*lunch*
Noon 12:30	*prepare for class* *class*	*prepare for class* *class*
1:00 1:30		
2:00 2:30	↓	↓
3:00 3:30	*commute home* *jog*	*commute home* *jog*
4:00 4:30	*study*	↓
5:00 5:30	↓	*go to store*
6:00 6:30	*dinner*	*dinner*
7:00 7:30	*study*	*dishes* *study*
8:00 8:30	↓	↓ *TV*
9:00 9:30	*laundry*	↓
10:00 10:30	*sleep*	*laundry* *study*
11:00 11:30		↓
Midnight 12:30		*read*
1:00 1:30		*sleep*

you that the diverse activities in your life will all get a guaranteed amount of time and that work on your project will not condemn you to a life of solitude and drudgery.

- You'll realize how little time there is in your life that is really available for work on your project. This will encourage you to start early and work on it more frequently.

How to Keep a Schedule

Fiore suggests the following rules for filling out and sticking to your schedule. First, make copies of the schedule on the following page.

1. Schedule as many nonwork and nonstudy activities as you can. This will give you a realistic idea of the time you actually do have to study or complete your project. Only schedule:

- Time that you have absolutely committed—sleeping, eating, meetings, commuting, classes, appointments, etc.
- Social commitments
- Exercise and play

For every thirty-minute period you actually study, darken a square on your schedule.

2. Fill in your studying time only after you have completed at least thirty minutes of quality work. Tally up the time you spent on your project at the end of each day.

3. After each thirty-minute period of quality work, reward yourself with a break or switch to a more enjoyable activity.

4. Always leave one complete day a week for leisure, fun, and chores.

5. Before you go to any leisure or social activity, allow thirty minutes of uninterrupted time to work on your project.

After you fill in the spaces for your previously committed time and your leisure and social activities, notice how much blank space is available to work on your school studies. Is it more than you imagined? Less? A lot less? You may want to juggle the amount of time you spend with friends or watching TV with the amount of time you have left over for school. But remember not to cut out all extracurricular activities. Fun and play are important—in fact, they are essential to a less stressful life. Any schedule that can be adhered to will have ample amounts of both.

Weekly Schedule

	Monday	Tuesday	Wednesday	Thursday	Friday	Saturday	Sunday
7 AM							
8 AM							
9 AM							
10 AM							
11 AM							
Noon							
1 PM							
2 PM							
3 PM							
4 PM							
5 PM							
6 PM							
7 PM							
8 PM							
9 PM							
10 PM							
11 PM							
Total study hours							

Sample Weekly Schedule

	Monday	Tuesday	Wednesday	Thursday	Friday	Saturday	Sunday
7 AM	shower and breakfast	————————————————→				sleep	sleep
8 AM	commute to school prepare for class	gym	commute to school prepare for class	gym	commute to school prepare for class		
9 AM	history class	commute home	history class	commute home	history class		
10 AM							newspaper
11 AM	lunch w/Kathy	lunch / prepare for class	commute home / lunch	lunch / prepare for class	lunch / commute to work	gym	
Noon	bio lab	biology class		commute to school	work	lunch	lunch
1 PM				biology class		garden and	
2 PM		prepare for class		prepare for class		housework	
3 PM	commute	English class	commute to work / work	English class			
4 PM	dr. appt						
5 PM	commute home dinner	commute home		commute home	commute home		
6 PM		dinner		dinner	dinner w/Mike	walk with Ted	dinner
7 PM	study with Sara and Kim		commute home dinner				
8 PM						movie	TV *Mad About You*
9 PM							*Masterpiece Theater*
10 PM	TV news	————————————————→					
11 PM	sleep	———————————————————————→					
Total study hours	3 ½ Hrs	4 Hrs	4 Hrs	3 ½ Hrs	1 Hr		2 ½ Hrs

Weekly totals

English ■ 5½ Hrs

history ▤ 7½ Hrs

biology ▨ 5½ Hrs

As you work to complete your goal, mark off each half-hour block of time *after* you have actually studied for that amount of time. You may want to use different colors for each subject. This will give you an even clearer understanding of where your time is going, and what you are accomplishing.

Time Management Tips

Break down big projects into small steps. You can suddenly feel overwhelmed and terrified when faced with any project for which you can't immediately imagine the exact procedure. When you take the big, complex, frightening whole and start to break it down into smaller, clear, and logical steps, the entire undertaking can seem more manageable. For instance, studying for a history final may seem daunting. There was so much material covered in the semester, and some of it you haven't read yet, and you were absent for several classes and didn't get those notes. However, you can break this project down into many simple steps that would clarify exactly what needs to be done. A list of these steps might look something like this:

1. *The test will cover chapters 1 through 22. As a first step, I need to review the notes I took for chapters 1 through 18.*

2. *I'll need to skim and take notes on chapters 19 through 22. Three weeks before the test I'll take one week to do so. I will complete a chapter a day and have two days extra for finishing up.*

3. *I'll also need notes for the two classes I missed in April. I'll ask Karen tomorrow if I can make a copy of her notes for those two days and for the last four chapters. Although I'll use her notes as a guide for the last four chapters, I know that writing and reciting notes is the best way to memorize material.*

4. *Two weeks before the test I'll reserve two and a half hours a day for reviewing. I'll review two chapters a day for a total of an hour and a half. When I review these chapters, I will:*

   a. *Recite the notes I took on the chapters*

   b. *Make sure I know the vocabulary words*

   c. *Answer the questions at the end of the chapter*

5. *I'll also spend an hour a day going over two weeks worth of class notes. I'll do this by:*

   a. *Reading through the notes and underlining points, questions, and data that I know to be important*

   b. *Reciting facts, figures, and lists from the notes*

6. *Sticking to this time frame will give me three days before the final to go over areas, questions, points, or lists that I don't feel confident I know yet. During this time I will review all past quizzes, tests, and other graded material.*

Focus on one thing at a time. Although the project of studying for this exam originally seemed enormous, after you broke it down into steps, you knew exactly what you needed to do with each day. Staying focused on each task as you do it will further reduce the likelihood of becoming overwhelmed. This means that, as you review each chapter, your thoughts and attention are directed only on that chapter. When your attention veers off onto anything else, as soon as you notice it, bring your focus back to the one chapter you are working on. Studying one chapter at a time is perfectly manageable. You've probably done it many times before. It's exactly the same thing you've been doing all semester.

Learning to use your spare time. Everyone has portions of his or her day that seem to be eaten up by the mechanics of life—a half hour on the bus to get to school, fifteen minutes in line at the bank, or forty-five minutes at the doctor's office. You may think, erroneously, that these smaller bits of time can't really be used for anything important, and so you're content to fritter them away. The truth is that there are many parts of any project that can be accomplished in short spurts of time, such as memorizing lists, planning strategies, or reciting facts and vocabulary words.

Procrastinators often have the view that if they can't sit down and finish their project in one sitting, then it's not worth sitting down at all. However, there are many small, critical parts of any project that can be completed in shorter stretches of time. Making an agreement with yourself to spend two and a half hours a day studying for a test doesn't mean you need one, large two-and-a-half-hour chunk to do it in. And breaking the task into smaller pieces makes the project seem less formidable. There actually is a built-in end in sight—the proverbial light at the end of the tunnel. You will find that there are many critical pieces in any project that can be addressed in short fifteen- to thirty-minute intervals.

Setting time limits. Before you begin work on any project, be sure you have clearly set a time when you will stop. Make this stopping time clear and unmoveable by writing it down. Then, once you have established the time to stop, make sure you stick to it. When you quit working at a designated stopping time, you are always leaving your project with a sense of accomplishment. You have completed exactly what you set out to do. You have been successful. It wasn't difficult.

You are encouraged to return tomorrow and have another successful experience.

Conversely, if you tell yourself that you will work for half an hour and then continue to work for another hour beyond that, you will always feel that you have to work a much longer time than you originally set out to. Even though you set a time limit before you begin, you already have seen that this limit is really meaningless. You may start to feel dread at the prospect of working on your project because you know you may be ensnared by it for hour after hour. Then, you may start putting off work on it until you "feel more like it," or until you "have more time." When you work past your designated stopping time, you are reinforcing the habit of procrastination.

Make your schedule flexible. Everyone knows that life often doesn't go exactly as planned. Vehicles break down, books disappear, printer paper runs out, and your favorite relatives (who you never see) suddenly show up on your doorstep. If you schedule your time so tightly that every minute is accounted for, you won't have enough slack to take care of the unexpected parts of life. Allow yourself a little leeway. Acknowledge that, despite your good intentions, your time may be taken up in ways that you have not even imagined yet, and plan accordingly.

Taking Action

No matter how long you've put off working on any project, the moment you actually start to do something toward solving that task, all procrastination comes to an end—at least momentarily. If you haven't gotten around to doing your class reading assignments for whatever reason, the moment you pick up your text and read the first word, weeks of procrastination can stop right there. You don't have to feel like it. You don't have to be ready. You just have to pick up the book, find the right page, and read.

It sounds so simple. But let's face it—if it were really simple, you wouldn't have procrastinated in the first place. Irrational as they are, your thoughts, emotions, and actions are trying to save you from an imagined, potentially frightening or disastrous experience. Taking action will become easier if you first examine the thoughts and feelings you actually have, and then, however subtly, change them. The following techniques will help to keep you focused on the importance of the task, and then put to rest the irrational thoughts and feelings that are keeping you from doing it.

Post your goal. Earlier in this chapter you wrote down your goal and the ten most crucial reasons to reach it. You then made several copies of this list and posted it in the areas where you will see it during the day. Now, whenever you notice yourself putting off starting work, read this list. Even though working on your task seems awful or scary or momentarily unimportant, this list should remind you of the consequences of not working on this task. If you don't want to study for the upcoming test, ask yourself if you can reach your career goals without doing well on this test. And, if you can't, what will your life be like without reaching your goal. Keeping this in mind at crucial moments will help you get past the aversion you feel to working on your assignment.

Focus on your thoughts. As chapter 3 showed, the irrational thoughts and mistaken beliefs that underlie your sense of anxiety over performing certain tasks all have to do with wrong information that your thoughts are giving you. It is important to catch each misinforming thought as it happens and replace it with a more truthful statement. When you figure out what exactly the truth is and look at it straight on, it will be much more difficult to momentarily ease your anxiety by procrastinating.

All you have to do is start. Working on any project is really a series of beginnings. If you can get yourself to physically sit down and concentrate on the task often enough, then you will eventually get to the end of it. You don't have to worry about whether you're working fast enough, or whether you'll be able to remember the right facts at a later date, or what the overall outcome will be. All you have to do is start the work, over and over and over again. At least 90 percent of the battle is getting yourself to sit down and focus on your task.

You may never feel like it. Many procrastinators believe that they're waiting for their feelings to "catch up" to the task. They may think they're waiting until they *want* to do it, or until they feel some kind of desire toward the task. Some may feel as though they're waiting for brilliance or inspiration. Others think that they need to feel more ready or less scattered and otherwise occupied before they embark on a task. And many think that they cannot start a task until they feel either no fear, or at least less fear, than they currently feel.

The truth is, you may never feel ready. Or, even if you do feel ready sometimes, you probably won't feel ready to work on your project as often as you need to in order to finish it. Regardless of what your feelings are telling you, you need to be able to sit yourself down at your desk with your books in front of you and give as much attention as you can to your project. As you develop this ability to sit down and start, you will find that the feelings you thought you needed to wait for will actually materialize once you begin to put forth an effort.

Start out imperfectly. Some people find it difficult to start class assignments because they feel that every little step along the way needs to be perfect. Having this expectation puts an added pressure on them that makes any progress incredibly slow, regardless of how much time they actually work on the project. One way to fight this tendency is to blatantly start out with an imperfection.

By purposefully incorporating an error into your work, you automatically erase any hope of making your assignment perfect. The error needn't be something glaring. A small mistake often can be enough to let you feel that the pressure to be perfect has diminished. If you are writing a paper, you could make an error in the language that you use. Or, you could consistently misspell a word throughout the text. Make an agreement with yourself that you are going to turn this paper in, mistake and all, no matter what. Even if prefabricating an error makes you feel somewhat uncomfortable, its value will be greater than your discomfort. The mistake you always try to avoid at any cost has already been made. Perfection is no longer an issue. You may now feel a little more free to create, and a little less afraid to experiment.

Make it rewarding. Keeping in mind that completing schoolwork now increases a person's chances of getting a good job in the future can be a way of keeping your mind on what's important. However, this realization still often fails to motivate habitual procrastinators to start and finish their work on time. If a reward is to compel you to action, it has to be both well defined and instantly gratifying. A small reward, perhaps a movie at nine o'clock tonight, may often be more motivating than a possible internship four years down the road.

When you have a large task in front of you, you may tend to avoid working on it because your imagination envisions hours, days, months of loneliness and isolation as you toil away in your study. If, instead, working on a project conjures up images of short periods of effort punctuated by numerous pleasurable activities, you are much more likely to approach your work often and with enthusiasm.

Procrastinators often feel that no matter how much headway they make toward the completion of a project, they still haven't accomplished enough to deserve any kind of positive reinforcement. The truth is that you deserve a reward every time you sit down and actually begin work on your assignment. One way to reward yourself is to keep and fill in the schedule as explained earlier in this chapter. And, always remember to do something nice for yourself after a preset period of work—say every thirty or sixty minutes. It doesn't need to be something big, just something that you will find enjoyable. Think of the small things you would like that you otherwise wouldn't give yourself—perhaps a nice walk, or an ice cream cone, or a hot bath in the middle of the day—and allow yourself this pleasant experience *after* you have completed a predetermined period of work. Coupling work that usually would make you feel anxious with a feeling of pleasure will help to change your overall outlook towards the task.

One technique that psychologists often use to help procrastinators start a task is called *sandwiching*. Work on the anxiety-producing task is strategically placed in between two enjoyable events. If you're dreading studying for a test, you could schedule your study session between meeting a friend for coffee and watching an hour of television. Your mind can then look forward to the things you enjoy, thereby easing the sense of dread you may feel about starting your project. You may feel that the work you would rather avoid is simply a way of passing time between two pleasurable events. It is important that preset time limits be established and adhered to for this technique to work well.

Keeping track of your progress. You won't be able to tell whether your study habits are improving unless you keep track of exactly how much studying you do each day. Make several copies of your schedule. Post one in the place where you usually study, one in the room where you spend most of your time, and carry one with you. As you complete each half-hour period of studying, fill in the square that indicates this. Count the time you spend studying each day and compare that with the amount of time you intended to study. Keep your eye on upcoming deadlines and periodically evaluate whether the amount of time you are studying each day will allow you to complete your assignments on time.

You can tolerate the intolerable. When you procrastinate, you are in reality choosing the short-term goal of not feeling a certain discomfort over the long-term goal of expending effort and ending up with a valuable reward. The moment you feel the queasy, uncomfortable sensation of having to do something you're not at ease with, your mind starts to invent all sorts of chatter designed to make you feel that it's really all right to quit.

For instance, you might find yourself thinking, "I can't stand this," when actually the truth is that you are "standing it" quite well. Or you might say, "I'm under too much stress. I need to ease up," or "I hate this so much that I can't do it." These kinds of statements serve as signposts pointing you to the nearest exit.

If at this time you believe the content of your thoughts, you are in danger of turning a challenge that might stretch you emotionally and mentally into a problem that you what to avoid. But meeting challenges in your life is one way in which you grow. Without that growth you stay exactly the same as you are with exactly the same limitations. So, realize that in these moments of stress, your habitual thoughts are not your friends. They are going to tell you the same old things and lead you into the same old patterns of behavior.

If you want to, you can choose to have a different behavior. When you find yourself saying, "I can't ... I don't want to ... It's too hard ..." notice that the moments between these thoughts aren't really too hard at all. They're just moments—there's you, some books, some paper, and some thoughts. They're really not too different from most of your other moments except for those thoughts that are telling you that it's too tough, that you don't feel like doing this, that you would rather do something less demanding. First consider what you'll lose by not following through. Then stop considering completely, put your attention back on your work, and get on with it.

7

Learning How to Learn

As a child, you learn whenever a certain thing stimulates your interest. If something captures your imagination and curiosity, your attention becomes so focused on that specific thing that you can usually remember or understand it almost effortlessly. But once you enter the formal educational system, you're required to learn at least some information that you find uninteresting. Kids in grade school often report that they like school fine, but are having trouble with one area—perhaps it's subtraction or spelling—something that they just aren't interested in.

The amount of this uncompelling information multiplies as you continue through the higher grades. What was once an uninteresting moment or two during your grade-school day can, by the time you're in college, mushroom into a whole list of required classes that leave you unexcited and unmoved. Not only does the sheer amount of information now become daunting, but your drive, interest, and attention tend to fade in and out. When test time rolls around, it seems as though you have a big pile of information in front of you that you'll never, ever be able to commit to memory. And, if you've ever failed a test, or even just didn't do as well as you wanted to, you may have already learned to have fearful or panicky thoughts and feelings at the mere thought of taking a test.

These are the conditions that make learning how to study a necessity. By following a set of studying techniques, you can learn how to read and remember large amounts of information, even when it's information you feel somewhat indifferent to. The study skills discussed in this chapter will help you to:

- Calm down panicky thoughts and bodily sensations

- Keep your mind on the material you're studying, not on your emotions

- Figure out what information is important (that means the information that will actually be on the test)

- Remember the information you've studied

- Recall the information you've studied when you are actually taking the test

By mastering these study skills, you'll be able to approach a test with a higher level of confidence. And the more confident you are, the less fear you will feel.

Staying Focused

You need to be able to focus your attention on any information long enough for your brain to retain it. This is true regardless of the form in which the information is presented. Attention operates in waves, or spurts. When you focus on an object, you can maintain a constant stream of attention for a limited time, but eventually thoughts unrelated to the original object will enter your mind. At this point, you have to make a conscious effort to return your attention to the object you're concentrating on. In the course of performing a task that requires concentration, your attention rises from the task, and then, as you recognize the attentional shift, returns to the task many, many times. How often this occurs depends on three variables:

1. Your natural ability to hold a one-pointed focus. This will vary from person to person depending on the way he or she learned to pay attention during childhood.

2. Your interest in the task you are doing. When you're fascinated by an object, you can fix your attention on it for a longer period of time than you could if you were merely curious about the object, or completely indifferent to it.

3. Your emotional state at the time. When you experience an emotion—anger, fear, love, excitement, worry, or whatever—your attention will be repeatedly drawn to the thoughts and bodily sensations related to that emotion.

Learning to concentrate more fully on material that you are either reading, watching, or listening to means that you'll need to become conscious of the thoughts that lead to your lapses of attention as they occur. With this in mind, let's look at how your mind works when it's drawn away from what you should be learning.

The Nature of Distraction

What leads your attention away from your object of concentration is almost always a thought. You may hear your neighbor's stereo through your bedroom wall, you may glance quickly at someone who walks into the room, or you may wriggle your toes when your foot falls asleep, but none of these events in itself actually derails your train of thought. Instead, it is the thought you have about the event that brings your concentration to a halt. Hearing your neighbor's music doesn't distract you. Rather, it's the thought "That music's annoying" or "That music's too loud" or "I like that music" that pulls your attention away. Feeling pins and needles in your feet doesn't distract you; it's the thought about how uncomfortable that sensation feels that derails your attention. And it isn't an added presence in the room that draws your attention. It's the thought, "Who is that?"

You'll realize this is true if you think back to the times in your life when you've been so wrapped up in what you were doing that nothing could interrupt you. Almost everyone has had this experience. Perhaps you were watching your favorite movie, or making out with someone you loved, or shooting a basketball in a tie game. Your thoughts stay steady when you are doing something that you feel really involved in. And most of the thoughts you have then will relate to the object of your focus.

Types of Distractions

Thoughts that arise and interrupt your attention fall into one of two categories. Noise and activities in your environment that attract your attention are called *external distractors*. Thoughts, feelings, and bodily sensations that demand your attention are called *internal distractors*. Often, when your attentional flow is interrupted, it is due to a combination of both internal and external elements. For instance, if you're nervous about not being able to learn the material that you need to study for a test, the internal distractors of these nervous thoughts leave your mind ready to look at practically any event in your environment as an excuse for taking a break from studying—the activity that's at the core of your anxiety.

External Distractors

When you put your attention on any activity or thing in your immediate surroundings, you become distracted from your fearful thoughts and this briefly eases your anxiety. The fact that your anxious feelings do let up a bit encourages your brain to repeat this type of attentional lapse. Any activity, or thought, or thing can serve as the sought-after distraction. However, noise is the all-time best external attention getter.

Any sound has the ability to grab your attention even though your eyes are staying on the page and your thoughts are trying tenaciously to comprehend the material. Whether it's a sound as loud as a jackhammer outside your window, or something as soft as a whisper from across a library table, a noise can pull your attention repeatedly with the nagging insistence of a mosquito buzzing around your ear. And, if you have reached a place in your studying that's difficult and you're progressing more slowly, any noise can draw your attention as your level of frustration rises. You may be tempted to think that the noise, especially an ongoing or repetitive one, is the source of your frustration. But, as previously noted, when your mind is absorbed, sound won't interfere with your stream of thought.

Internal Distractors

Internal distractors fall into one of two groups: thoughts and bodily sensations. When you're feeling anxious about how you'll do on an upcoming test, or whether you'll pass a particular course, you're already dealing with both of these. Your mind will be thinking thoughts about how you won't be able to remember anything at the critical time, or how you're not good enough, or smart enough, or any of a number of other thoughts about how you won't be able to succeed. These are called *negative self-statements*. Again, these thoughts occur because you have developed a habit of imagining the worst in certain critical situations. The original thought behind this strategy was something like "If I don't pass this test I'll feel horrible. If I don't even try, I'll avoid the terrible feeling of having failed. Then I won't feel as bad." You think that if you can imagine the worst, you can prepare for it, or avoid it entirely. Refer back to chapter 3 if you'd like to review this topic.

Your body responds to these negative self-statements by producing all of the various physical sensations discussed in chapter 2: tense muscles, quickened heart rate, shallow breathing, and so on. In effect, your body is getting ready to flee from what it perceives as a dangerous situation. And in turn, as you try to make sense of your physical sensations, your thoughts become more agitated. This interaction of thoughts and corresponding bodily sensations is an emotional response. In this case, the emotional response is that of fear.

Here's an example of how the fear mind/body connection might work: Julia has a math test scheduled for next Monday. Even though she has almost a week to study for it, she finds herself becoming alarmed from time to time. The thought "Oh, no, I won't be able to remember anything" keeps invading her mind. This mental dread, accompanied by momentary feelings of panic, continuously captures her attention during study sessions. She imagines a time, a couple of years ago, when she went into a test feeling confident and, although she passed, she had not done the A work she felt she was capable of. She has had the experience of not remembering something when it was necessary, and now, in an effort to avoid reliving that painful situation, her brain is warning her that the same danger may be present again.

This thought, however, is not an accurate reflection of reality. She might sit down with the test and remember everything. Or, more likely, she will probably remember most things, but forget a few. Nonetheless, her mind is telling her that the danger of remembering nothing exists, and in response, her body prepares itself to flee from the situation with the appropriate physical responses. When Julia realizes that she is afraid of taking this test, she attempts to understand the nature of this fear and produces more negative self-statements which, in turn, produce more fearful bodily sensations. Once the cycle of fear has begun, it continually escalates.

The Most Important Study Technique: Tracking Your Thoughts

When doubts enter your brain, your attention may suddenly leap off the page and run with the fearful sensations in your body. As you try to make sense of these panicky feelings, you may find yourself actually believing your thoughts—that you'll never get through the course, memorize the material, or get the paper done on time, and, besides, you didn't really want to have this career anyway. You'd really rather be a _____ (fill this in with anything that seems much less challenging, and therefore less threatening). When you start to believe your fearful thoughts, you can be sure you're on the road that leads away from success, personal growth, emotional fulfillment, and inner satisfaction. Remember: Panicky thinking is a habit—not a reflection of reality.

The first and most important study skill you'll learn is to recognize that moment when your mind leaves the subject matter it's trying to absorb. This task is much more difficult than it sounds. Your mind's continuous chatter is so automatic that much of the time you don't notice when your thoughts jump from one track to another. Even when your thoughts engender fear and anxiety, you often remain unaware of the actual thought and only notice your feelings as they become frightening or troubling in some way.

Simply becoming aware of the fearful thought/sensation/emotion habit more than likely won't cause your panicky sensations to ease up.

This kind of negative thinking took you many years to master. In order to change it, you'll need time to create some new and different successful experiences. But in order to have a successful experience, you'll need to walk on your own two feet right through the circumstances that scare you, and this means that you'll need to find a way to function successfully in the world while still experiencing the sensations of fear and panic. You can learn to tolerate feelings of fear, even feelings of extreme fear, and still function well and successfully in the real world (including all learning institutions and classrooms).

In part, the phenomenon of not knowing your own thoughts is due to the abbreviated way in which thoughts often occur. Rarely do people think in complete sentences. The memory of a single word or a fleeting image of a past event can open a floodgate of memories or plans along with the feelings you associate with them. And by the time you notice that your mood has changed, the initiating thought has often drifted into oblivion.

You can observe the jumpy, scattered nature of your thought process by doing this simple exercise:

> Sit comfortably on the floor or in a chair. Take a moment to relax your body (see chapter 2). Then put all of your attention on the part of your abdomen that goes in and out as you breathe. Stay attuned to the physical sensations as your abdomen rises and falls with each breath. When a thought enters your awareness, instead of getting wound up in the subject matter, notice that you are thinking, assign a number to the thought, and then return your attention to the rising and falling of your abdomen. Continue to count your thoughts for five minutes.

People who try this exercise for the first time are often amazed at their inability to keep their attention fixed for any length of time, and at the multitude of thoughts that scamper through their head within a relatively short time. Did you feel that you caught each thought as it occurred, or were you thinking for a while before you actually became conscious of it? The odds are fairly good that, most of the time, you missed the actual shift when you lost awareness of your breath and got all wrapped up in your thinking.

When you learn to notice that your thoughts have left the subject matter and are contemplating unrelated topics (which might include a good deal of negative self-talk), you can choose to disengage your attention from the content of your current thoughts and return it to your book or notes. Learning how to concentrate is not a matter of willpower.

It's the repetitive act of catching your mind when it strays, then returning it to the thing on which you were originally concentrating. Even when something as compelling as thoughts of doom or feelings of dread are drawing your attention, you can always choose to disengage your awareness from your fear (or anything else) and return it to the material you need to learn.

How to Operate Your Mind While Studying for a Test

Following are several methods that, when practiced, will help you study, learn, and remember even when you're experiencing fear. They are designed to help you focus your attention on the material at hand and keep your body's nervous system calm.

Take a Step Back

When your thoughts don't want to stay on the material in front of you, every five minutes or so stop studying and see if you can track what your thoughts have been doing. This will help you develop the habit of noticing when your mind wanders off and what it is that you are thinking. Have you been preparing for the worst? Dreading the future? Are you feeling anxious or fearful? Where do you feel the fear in your body? Take just a moment to ask yourself these questions, then return your attention to your books and notes.

Disengage

Whenever you notice yourself thinking thoughts unrelated to your studying, note to yourself their general content. When you do this, remove the word "I" from this labeling process. Instead of saying, "I'm thinking about how afraid I'll be when I take this test tomorrow," say "There's a thought about being nervous tomorrow" or "Thinking about being nervous . . ." This will help you create a space between "yourself" and the content of your thinking. Once you've noticed your thought, disengage your attention from it, however compelling the content seems, and return it to the subject you're studying.

Repeat This Process Over and Over and Over Again

Whenever you notice your attention has wandered, disengage it from your thinking and return it to your study material. Within the course of a studying session, you may have feelings such as nervousness, boredom, restlessness, fear, and panic. These feelings are expected and natural. They will come and go. But it is quite possible to allow your body to experience these sensations while you refocus your concentration on something else. So, whenever your emotions become distracting, notice this fact, then consciously return your attention to the subject of study.

Set Aside Worry Time

If thoughts related to a particular issue continue to resurface, make an agreement with yourself to set aside ten minutes every hour to focus on these specific thoughts. If you're having worried thoughts, sit down and worry for ten minutes. If you're having catastrophic thoughts, sit down and catastrophize for ten minutes. Notice any feelings and sensations as they occur, or as they change into different feelings and sensations. When the allotted worry time is over, disengage your attention and return to your studying. Remember, once you've made this agreement with yourself, be sure to keep it. You need to know that you can count on yourself.

Stop Your Thoughts

If at times you feel as though your mind is racing and thoughts are continuously interrupting your concentration, try yelling "stop." If at all possible, yell it out loud. If not, place a rubber band around your wrist and snap it as you mentally yell the word "stop." Then, immediately return your attention to your book or notes. Repeat this procedure as often as you need to.

Talk Yourself through the Assignment

Experiments have shown that students who study out loud retain four times more information than students who study silently. When you read or study silently, all the thoughts inside your head, regardless of their content, are equally as loud. If you study in an environment that allows you to say every word you read or write out loud, the thoughts you have about the material you're studying will become much louder than all your other thoughts. You may want to stop at the end of each paragraph or section and, in your own words, summarize aloud what you have just read. Studying with your voice is the most effective technique you can use for implanting facts into your memory.

Ask for Help

If you're working on material that you're having difficulty with, as your frustration level rises, your thoughts will more rapidly spin off onto other things. Rather than wasting time spinning your mental wheels, ask for help—regardless of what the difficulty is. If you find the thought of asking for help intimidating, first remember that there

are no stupid questions—everyone, sooner or later, needs help to understand something—and then ask the least scary person you can think
of to help you. You may want to approach a classmate or tutor instead
of the instructor. The more often you ask for help, the more you'll
realize that no one will think you are silly and your confidence and
ability to do this will grow.

Get Out of Your Head

Sometimes you get so wound up with your fears, concerns, plans,
and the events in your life, that your mind seems to bring up the same
thoughts over and over again. Often, the best way to handle this is to
get your attention out of your head and into your body. You can do
this by practicing any of the exercises in chapter 2. Aerobic exercise—activity that elevates you heart rate for at least twenty minutes—is also
a good way to calm down your mind.

Give Your Mind a Break

When you're really struggling with the material and you don't
seem to be making any progress, take a break and give your mind a
rest. Go for a walk, or see a movie, or prepare yourself a nice meal.
As your mind focuses on other things, it will also, subconsciously, be
shuffling through the subject matter, trying to make sense of it. When
you return to your books and notes, you may perceive the concepts
more clearly.

How Memory Works

Your brain channels information to one of two different places—your
short-term memory and your long-term memory. Your short-term memory stores small amounts of information for a limited period of time.
This is the type of memory that most people use when they sit down
and read a book for recreation. It has been shown that 50 percent of
all the material people read is forgotten by the time they've stopped
reading. And after twenty-four hours, most people will only retain 20
percent of the information that they read only the day before.

When you have a piece of information that you'll want to recall
days, weeks, or even years later, you want to be able to route it to
your long-term memory. Once information enters here, it never leaves.
To get information to your long-term memory, a thought needs to wear
down a path, or a *neural trace,* to that information. Each time you remember a piece of information, the path to it becomes more worn and
easier to follow. The information, then, becomes easier to find. Obviously the key to remembering information easily on a test is to review
that information in your memory many times before the test.

Getting the Most Out of Class

When you simply listen to a speech or lecture, regardless of how strongly you focus, that information will usually be stored in your short-term memory. This means that a full 50 percent of it will have evaporated from your brain within an hour! And within twenty-four hours, the amount of the material that you'd be able to recall at will would be very, very small. Without notes, you would have no way of retrieving it.

A complete and thorough set of notes can become your most valuable textbook. Often, instructors fill their lectures with the facts that they feel are most important—which is usually the information that they will put on the test. It is not unusual to see a test in which 80 percent or more of the material covered comes from lectures. In classes like these, you can see that it's quite possible to pass the test by taking a comprehensive set of notes and studying it well.

Note taking is also a tremendously effective way of keeping your attention on the lecture. By connecting your hearing, sight, thinking, and hand coordination, you become completely involved in the classroom experience. It's practically impossible to space out or daydream when your brain is devoted to this task.

Tips on Note Taking

The following techniques will help you record your classroom notes more effectively:

Sit in the front of the classroom. There are several reasons to sit as close to the lecturer as you can. First of all, when you sit where you're likely to be noticed, it's much more embarrassing, and therefore difficult, to fall asleep or daydream. You'll also be in the best position to hear every word and see everything written on the blackboard. And there will be virtually no people, objects, or noises between you and the instructor that could grab at your attention. By sitting in the front of the class you are making the statement to yourself, your instructor, and the rest of the world, that you are interested, committed, and ready to learn.

Take a mini-review. Arrive at your class early and skim over your notes from the previous class or any reading you were assigned for that week. Write down any points you want to have clarified. Give your brain a chance to warm up and get in sync with the subject.

Leave out unimportant words. Since, in general, people can speak much more quickly than they can write, you need to find ways to speed up the note-taking process. One way to do this is to leave out all the words that are unimportant to the meaning of the notes. Write your notes as though you were sending a message by telegraph and had to pay for every word. Forget rules of grammar. If, for instance, a lecturer says: "The village, which usually consisted of a number of scattered hamlets, was the lowest administrative level in the bureaucratic hierarchy," you could convey this by writing:

The village which was scattered hamlets was lowest administrative level.

Use graphics and abbreviations. Using word abbreviations and graphic symbols will speed up your note taking. Bracket or circle concepts that belong together. Star or underline important phrases. Use arrows to show cause/effect relationships, or to replace the words *became, produced, turned into,* and so on. Equal signs can replace the words *was, were, is,* and *are.* When you're first learning to use these symbols, be sure to assign the same meaning to each symbol each time you use it. Using these symbols will quickly become second nature. The sentence about the administrative level of the village could be further abbreviated like this:

Village (scattered hamlets) = lowest admin. level

Outline. Taking notes is like trying to see the whole puzzle as you look at one piece at a time. Although the organizational structure of the lecture might not be easily recognized at any given point, remember that the instructor is most likely lecturing from notes that he has written in outline form. The structure is present, it's just a matter of seeing the forest through all the words. When you outline, you're adding visual clues to designate which points are major and which are supporting ones. This will add a clarity to your notes, which you otherwise might find confusing when you go back to review.

Become a funnel. When you take notes, know that your sole purpose for being in the classroom is to collect everything the instructor says and to funnel it onto your paper. Suspend all judgment, debate, and nit-picking. Whenever you notice your mind chattering about something else, let it go. Don't think, ponder, or reflect (you'll have plenty of time for that later). Don't paraphrase or rearrange the instructor's words (not only is this time consuming, but often instructors like to see their own words on tests). When you write down your own thoughts or questions, be sure to mark these clearly so that you know that they are yours. Write down everything—don't view anything as too obvious. If the instructor is speaking too fast, don't stop in a fit of frustration. Capture what you can. Even fragments are better than nothing.

Don't skimp on paper. Leave a lot of space between ideas whenever you miss words or phrases, or when the instructor is speaking faster than you can write. This space will allow you to go back and fill in what you can after class. If you get lost or have questions, mark these places in your notes so that you'll be able to clarify the material later, making your set of notes more complete. Also, write on only one side of the paper. You can then organize and review your notes by spreading them out on a table or floor.

Stay alert during the final minutes. Often, instructors lose track of time and have to cram the final minutes of a lecture with a ton of information. Write particularly quickly during this time. Stay after class, if necessary, and continue filling in your notes until you have everything down that you can remember. Even though most instructors get the majority of their test material from their lecture notes, they seldom remember when a topic was barely touched upon in class because time was short.

Review notes as soon as you can. At your first opportunity, while your memory is still fresh (and remember that it doesn't stay fresh for long), go over your notes and fill in any gaps. Also, look for the organizational pattern. Without copying your notes over (this wastes time), see if you can add letters or numbers (if you haven't already) that will make the main points and subpoints pop out (as though you were superimposing the outline form on top of your notes). Make sure that all the main points are well marked.

No typing, no taping. Remember that the best way to imprint information into your long-term memory is to write it down, then recite it out loud. For this reason, typing notes and recording lectures are largely time-wasting activities. If you record a lecture, you'll need to relisten to it and take notes as you do! Typing up your notes accomplishes even less (since you already have them written down). Retyping may make them cleaner to look at, but this is one place where neatness doesn't really count for much. Your time would be better spent by making lists or flash cards and reciting this information over and over again.

Figuring Out What's Important

During a lecture, an instructor may behave in certain ways that will clue you in to which points seem important to him or her. Watching for, recognizing, and noting these cues may well make your studying much easier. Here is a list of things that will indicate when a topic may appear on a test:

Repetition. Instructors often repeat points that they regard as crucial. When this happens, be sure to mark it in your notes.

Writing on the board. Instructors seldom take time to write material on the board, or put it on an overhead projector, unless they view this information as important. In fact, quite often the purpose of presenting the information in writing is to give you time to write it down. So copy everything. Mark clearly which material you copied from the board and commit it to memory. Be sure to notice which words or phrases are underlined.

Referring to the notes. When instructors refer to their notes, it usually means they want to be sure that a specific point is made, or that they have included all the points they wanted to. Rarely is it to find interesting anecdotes or frivolous information. Any material that was covered immediately before or immediately after a brief note check is often very important. Be sure to mark this action in your notes.

Signal words. Certain introductory, transitional, and concluding phrases may signal which points or facts will appear on the test. Here is a list of phrases to watch for:

Enumeration
The three steps to ...
The five factors are ...

Summary words
In conclusion ...
To sum it up ...

Emphasis words
The most important part ...
Especially ...
Above all ...

Repetition
In a nutshell ...
In other words ...
What this all means is ...

Cause and effect
If ... then ...
As a result ...
Therefore ...

The instructor's clues. Most instructors aren't trying to shroud the important parts of their lectures in mystery. Quite often they will use key phrases that convey the importance of certain material. Some of these are

This may be on the test
Remember this
This is important

Animation. Instructors often test for material that they themselves find interesting. This interest can become apparent in the classroom when the instructor actually looks excited. He or she may talk more quickly or more loudly, or may use larger hand gestures, gesture more often, or in general appear more animated. If you notice this shift in behavior, mark it in your notes.

Getting the Most Out of
Reading Texts

You've already learned that when you sit down and read for pleasure, the information you take in is automatically stored in your short-term memory. So, if you just read your textbook, odds are that you won't retain much information. In order to remember the material beyond an hour, an afternoon, or a day or so, you need to take action to move it into your long-term memory.

Tips on Active Reading

The following instructions show you how to implant the information from your textbook into your brain:

1. Get an overview. Before you begin the actual reading, take a moment to skim the chapter and get an overview of the material you'll be covering. Read the table of contents to see how your assignment fits into the whole. Scan the chapter titles and the section headings and subheadings; see what they tell you about the nature of the topics you'll be reading about. Make a mental note of the areas that are familiar to you. Look for material that naturally arouses your curiosity and notice any parts that seem as though they might be particularly challenging. Look over any drawings, charts, graphs, and tables until you are familiar with their content. Information presented in these formats registers quickly and may make you feel familiar with the reading material.

Finally, take a few minutes to warm up your brain to the actual subject matter. One way to do this is by reading the short summary at the end of the chapter first, if the chapter does have a summary. Or, if you have some familiarity with the topic, call up whatever information you already know and roll it around your brain for a bit. Taking a minute to ease your understanding into a subject, instead of butting your thoughts up against it, will help you comprehend the material more quickly.

2. Make up questions. Before you begin reading, write down any questions that popped into your mind as you did your overview. What were you interested in? What was confusing? What seemed difficult, or vague and unclear?

Then, take a good look at the section titles and subtitles. As you do this, see if you can rearrange the words to form a question. For instance, if a subtitle reads "Genes and Behavior," your question could be "How do genes affect behavior?" Asking a question will give you something specific to look for as you read down each page.

3. Read. Now that you have previewed the material and have formulated questions that you want to answer, you're ready to actually begin reading. Before you turn to the first page and look at the first sentence, pick up a pen or highlighter and be prepared to mark up your book. As your eyes go down each page, highlight the important points and subpoints—you may want to use two different colors for this. Use restraint when you highlight. If too many points are marked, you'll have defeated the purpose of highlighting, which is to make the important material pop out.

Remember the question you formed out of each section's heading and look for the answer to it as you read. Briefly outline your answers on a separate piece of paper. Notice when the answers are confusing or different from what you expected. Ask the instructor to clarify anything you don't understand.

Whenever your attention starts to wander from your book to other things, simply drop the extraneous thoughts as you notice them and move your attention back to your book. If your thoughts won't stay steady, try making a check mark on a piece of scrap paper whenever you notice that you're thinking about something else. You may start out by quickly making a ton of check marks, but, as you continue, your thoughts will slow down and will tend to stay on the subject for longer stretches of time. Another way to capture wandering attention is to read out loud. This is especially helpful when the content of the material is difficult. Reading for shorter periods of time will also help you stay more focused.

Remember: The trick isn't to stop having thoughts unrelated to your reading; it's to shorten the length of time it takes to notice that you're thinking distracting thoughts and then move your attention back to your reading. In other words, you're speeding up your reaction time, and this takes practice.

---

4. Outlining. Stop reading after the end of each section. Review the material you've highlighted and the questions you've answered, then write an outline that includes this material. Use section and paragraph headings and subheadings for your main points. From this point on, you'll be using this outline to study from, so make it fairly detailed and complete. Taking a little more time to do this now will save you loads of time and effort later.

5. Recite. After you've read and outlined your assignment, use your outline as a guide and go through the main and supporting points of your reading and talk to yourself, preferably out loud, about them. One way to begin is to look at each major heading and then run through everything you can remember about that topic. When you're finished, look back at your outline and see what you got wrong or left out. After you've looked at this point on your outline a second time, recite the information again. When you can recite all the information under one heading, move on to the next point. Continue in this way until you reach the end of your outlined material.

Plan to start reciting your material within twenty-four hours after you've read it. Doing this will take the information in your short-term memory and move it into your long-term memory. If you wait longer than twenty-four hours, much of the material will have left your memory entirely and it'll take you valuable extra time to get it back. It'll be like starting over.

6. Review. Reviews need not be long and involved. As you continue with your reading throughout the term, every few days or so look over the notes you've taken on previous reading assignments. Recite the information once to make sure you still remember it. If you still have any questions, look up the answers, ask the instructor, or talk about your confusion with other classmates. If you conduct these brief reviews frequently, you'll already have retained much of the information by the time the test rolls around.

Remember: The more often you review a fact before a test, the more worn the path that leads to that fact will become in your memory.

---

7. Final Review. Before an exam, you'll want to gather all the outlines for the assignments you'll be tested on and review these materials as a whole. If you've kept up with your mini-reviews, you'll be surprised at how easy the final review will be. If you haven't been doing your mini-reviews, the final review will take up a lot more of your time.

Begin by dividing your lecture notes into sections. Read the outline for your lecture notes for the first section. Look and see what material from the text corresponds with it. Go back and look at any charts, graphs, or diagrams that contain pertinent information. Recite any information you don't feel confident you can remember. Go through the questions you've written for each section and answer them out loud.

If you're having trouble with a particular section, try rereading this material as though you were seeing it for the first time. You might find it helpful to do this out loud. Make a new outline. Sometimes when you approach a section as though you've never seen it before, it will suddenly start to make some kind of sense.

Figuring Out What's Important

It's a week before your biology midterm. You've surveyed all the material that you covered in the past half semester—both in class and reading. There are eight long chapters in your biology text, pages of lab notes, five articles from scientific magazines, and the notes you took on a film about wildlife preservation. Your instructor has said that all this material is fair game.

You've done all the work, but remembering everything seems impossible, no matter how long you study. How can you figure out exactly what questions you'll be asked on the test? The answer is, you can't! Well, not exactly, anyway. However, with a little preparation you can make a good, educated guess and be able to come closer to the actual questions than you ever thought possible. In order to make this educated guess, you need to lay a little groundwork at the beginning of the term. Here are some suggestions:

Keep a test question section. After each class and reading assignment, write out several possible test questions on a sheet of paper and file it in a separate section in your binder. Pretend that you are the instructor and ask yourself which information is key to the lesson you've just heard or studied.

Define the test. Sometime near the beginning of the term, ask the instructor to describe the test you'll be given on the material you're now covering. How long will it be? How many questions will be on it? What kind of questions? Essay? Multiple choice? Fill-in-the-blank? Will it be an open-book test? Can you use your notes? Calculators? And finally, ask something like, "What type of material will be covered?" This question is pointed, yet vague enough to elicit whatever information about the actual content that the instructor is willing to tell you. All instructors are different. Some will practically tell you the exact questions that will be on the exam. Others won't even discuss content. Find out how much your instructor is willing to hint at and take whatever he or she offers as very valuable information.

Pay attention to dual coverage. As a general rule, if a topic is covered in both your textbook reading and in class lectures, the odds are astronomical that this material will be on the test in some form. If a topic is covered in your lectures, but not in your reading, this tells you that the instructor thought it extremely important, and this, too, is likely to appear on a test. Material from your textbook that the instructor doesn't mention in class has the least likely chance of appearing on your test. (But since this isn't always the case, be sure to edit your reading material with care.)

Save all quizzes. Store all of your quizzes or other graded material with your list of possible test questions. Often instructors use quizzes as a way of preparing you for midterm and final exams. If a question is on a quiz, there is a good chance that it will reappear on a test.

Brainstorm. Get together with a group of students and brainstorm possible questions and topics that might appear on the test. If there is any significant question or area that you haven't considered up until now, it's likely that someone else will bring it up in a brainstorming session.

Look at the first test as a model. The first test you take from any given instructor will be the hardest. Often instructors use the same length, structure, and type of material on their tests throughout the entire term. After you take the first test, you'll better understand what type of information your instructor is likely to be looking for.

A Word about Cramming

Everyone's heard that cramming is a ineffective way to prepare for a test. When you cram, you memorize a lot of information very quickly. Usually you can retain this information for, at most, a couple of days, and then much of it fades away. The neural paths in your memory haven't been worn very deeply. Clearly, this is not the same as true learning. Anyone who has crammed for a midterm only to find that the information has completely evaporated by the time the final rolls around will attest to this.

If you are someone who hasn't gone to class all term, taken many notes, or even looked at your textbook, then cramming for the test won't help you at all. However, if you have attended most of your classes and have at least skimmed through your reading material, cramming might help you raise your grade from a C or D to a B level.

And let's face it—sooner or later life events clash with your academic needs, and everyone eventually has a test that he or she needs to cram for. With this in mind, here is the most effective way to infuse a maximum amount of information into your brain within a limited amount of time.

Step 1. Get a complete set of notes. If you've missed several classes, or even if you simply don't trust your note-taking ability, arrange to get a copy of a set of class notes, preferably from the best note taker in the class.

Step 2. Skim—don't read—the texts. Search for main topics and supporting facts, then write these down in outline form. Pay special attention to section headings and charts, diagrams, and graphs. These convey a lot of information very quickly. Don't get bogged down with this step. Use only about one quarter of the time you have to study to go over your text.

Step 3. Now put your books away and use only your notes for the rest of your studying—both the lecture notes and the ones you just took from your textbook. Go through both sets and put a big star (or use a highlighter, or a different color of ink) beside all the information that you feel fairly certain will be on the test. Then, go through your notes a second time and mark all the information that you think could possibly be on the test in yet another color. Successful cramming depends on making smart choices about what to memorize. You don't have time to memorize everything now. If you choose wisely, and are just a little lucky, you might retain the right facts long enough to get through the test.

Step 4. Start at the top of your notes again. Whenever you come to a portion that you marked as prime test material, stop and recite it, out loud, over and over again. Reciting is the quickest way you have of getting things to stick in your mind. When you think you know it, write it out. If you make mistakes when you write it, go back and recite it again. As soon as you can write it with an acceptable degree of accuracy, go on to the next material that you highlighted on your first pass through your notes. Only when you've recited everything you marked on the first pass do you start reciting the clumps of material marked on the second pass.

Remember: When you cram, you feel as though you're under increased pressure. Your anxiety level will rise even higher than it would normally. This means that you'll be more likely to give an incorrect answer during the test or blank out on a question completely. If you tend to experience test-taking anxiety under normal studying conditions, you should avoid cramming whenever possible.

Test-Taking Tips

The grade you get on any given test doesn't reflect your goodness, or your integrity as a human being. It isn't even a real indication of how smart you are, or of how much you learned in that class. It might reflect something about the length of time you put into preparing for a test. But, more often than not, getting a low test grade usually means that you haven't learned how to prepare for and take a test very well.

Since you're aware that you're prone to having anxious thoughts and feelings when you feel as though you have to perform, learning to keep your anxiety at a level at which you can function is as important as answering questions correctly. Below is a list of test-taking tips that will help you lower your anxiety level while maximizing your ability to accurately complete as much of the test as you can.

Watch your self-talk. From the moment you open your eyes on the day of the test, your thoughts will probably be chattering on about how scared you are and how your fear will keep you from doing well. Your task is to realize the meaninglessness of these thoughts. There might be a bit of truth to them. They might be completely false. Having critical or catastrophizing thoughts is not going to help you do any better on the test. They will only increase your anxiety level—and that's all they will do! When thoughts like these start to arouse fearful sensations in your body, don't look for the meaning in the thought. Instead, practice a relaxation technique immediately. If none come to mind, breathe deeply, low into your belly, while focusing on the physical sensation of your breath going in and out (see chapter 2).

Be on time. Lateness in and of itself will cause your anxiety level to rise. Arriving with time to spare will allow you to calm yourself with deep breathing or another relaxation technique.

Bring all the materials you'll need. In order to do this, you first need to know what exactly these materials are. Will you be using pencil or ink? If you will be using pencil, take several sharp ones with you. Can you use plain scratch paper? Will it be provided? What about a calculator? Blue book? Arriving at the test site with everything you'll need will add to your feeling of being well prepared for this test.

Avoid your fellow classmates. On the morning of a test, almost all classrooms are buzzing with the question "How much did you study for the test?" Everyone's either trying to think of all the topics they forgot to study, or bemoaning the fact that they didn't study enough. The thing to remember is that none of this conversation is of any use to anybody, and the only effect it serves is to increase everyone's general sense of fear and dread. You'll have plenty of time to socialize after the test. When you first arrive, sit off by yourself somewhere and, with clarity and purpose, look over a few of your class notes.

Act confident. Pretend you're playing the part of a very confident and adept individual. Assure yourself that you really do know the material and that taking this test is an opportunity, not a misery. Behaving in a calm manner will interrupt the formation of panicky thoughts and sensations. Acting confident will also nudge you toward an attitude that's more self-assured. To act as though you have confidence, simply do those things that confident people do:

- Assume the posture of someone who is calm and in control. Stand and sit with your back straight and your shoulders back. When appropriate, fold your hands calmly in your lap.

- Slow down. Move with dignity. Imagine what it's like to move at a leisurely pace. Avoid movements that you associate with being frantic or nervous.

- Avoid expressing your nervousness verbally. Don't whine or complain to your friends and family. Instead, replace nervous talk with the statement, "I'm going to study hard and do my best."

Take time to focus. Arrive at the test site early and take this time to really focus on something. If you can keep your mind steady as you review your notes, that's fine. However, if looking at your notes adds to your feeling of panic and dread, focus on an aspect of your environment—the shininess of the linoleum, the coolness of the desk seat, the humming of the fluorescent light. Try to put all of your attention on any one thing that is external to your thoughts and feelings.

Listen carefully to verbal instructions. Often you're so anxious to find out what questions are on the test that you eagerly pore over the test questions while the teacher's instructions fade into a drone in the background. These verbal instructions are important information. Listen to them.

Read all instructions slowly and read them twice. Students often spend needless time and energy responding to questions in a way that wasn't asked for, or leave out information that was required. Make sure you understand all the instructions completely before you begin.

Ask for clarification. Most instructors want to be fair and are quite willing to briefly discuss the type of material they are looking for.

If you're afraid you'll forget it, write it down fast. Whenever you have dates, formulas, vocabulary words, or lists of any kind that you feel you just crammed into your memory and might forget, write them down. As soon as you get the test, jot anything down that you want to remember either in the margin or on the back of the test questions.

Skim the test and budget your time. Familiarize yourself with the types of questions asked in each section. Consider the number of questions, how complex each question is, and how much each question is worth. Then figure out an appropriate amount of time to spend on each section. Be realistic. If a section of a hundred-point test is only worth twenty points, you don't want to spend 50 percent of your time on it.

Answer the easy questions first. You'll feel a sense of confident relief once you have a few questions under your belt. This is also a good way to warm up your thinking process. The longer you think about a specific subject, the more quickly the thoughts will materialize about that subject.

Don't panic when you don't know the answer. Try to think of the answer to each question as you read it. If nothing comes to mind right away, don't panic. Thinking is a process. Reading the question was only the first step in the process. The second step is to let the question percolate in your subconscious mind as you continue on to the next questions. When you've finished the questions that you know, go back to the questions you don't know. If nothing comes to mind when you reread a question:

- Look for hints in the other questions. Notice names, dates, or any other data that might jog your memory.

- Try to remember something the question is related to. Concentrate on a general theme and see if that will help any specific facts pop up.

- If you've tried everything and your memory is still blocked, start writing something. Pick a line of thinking that is as close to the subject as you can get and start writing. Write as much as you can think of, even if it isn't quite what the question asked for. Many instructors will give you partial credit for a decent try.

Use relaxation techniques and coping responses. Before the test, review all the coping responses discussed in this book. Pick out the two or three that work best for you and make an agreement with yourself to use these during the test if you feel you need to lower your anxiety level. When taking the test, if at any time you feel like your anxiety is about to overtake your ability to think and reason, stop for a minute or so and practice the appropriate relaxation technique or coping response. Use whatever one you've found calms you down most quickly.

Remember: It's perfectly normal for anyone to have panicky feelings during a test. Your anxiety level is most likely to rise when

   You enter the classroom

   You are first handed the test

   You read your first question

   You start a new section

   You run into a question you don't know the answer to

   You feel as though you're running out of time

Whenever your anxiety increases, take a deep breath. Take several breaths. And use whatever coping response will help.

Further Resources

Relaxation and Stress Reduction

Becker, Carol. 1987. *The Invisible Drama: Women and the Anxiety of Change.* New York: Macmillan.

Benson, Herbert. 1975. *The Relaxation Response.* New York: Morrow.

Bernstein, D., and T. Borkovec. 1973. *Progressive Relaxation Training: A Manual for Helping Professionals.* Chicago: Research Press.

Bry, Adelaide. 1978. *Visualization: Directing the Movies of Your Mind.* New York: Barnes and Noble.

Charlesworth, Edward A., and Ronald G. Nathan. 1984. *Stress Management: A Comprehensive Guide to Wellness.* New York: Atheneum.

Davis, Martha, Elizabeth R. Eshelman, and Matthew McKay. 1995. *The Relaxation & Stress Reduction Workbook.* 4th ed. Oakland, CA: New Harbinger Publications.

Gawain, Shakti. 1992. *The Creative Visualization Workbook.* Berkeley, CA: New World Library.

Geba, Bruno Hans. 1973. *Breathe Away Your Tension.* New York: Random House.

Haxthausen, Margit. 1987. *Body Sense: Exercises for Relaxation.* New York: Pantheon.

Jacobson, Edmund. 1942. *Progressive Relaxation.* Chicago: University of Chicago Press.

Kabat-Zinn, Jon. 1990. *Full Catastrophe Living: Using the Wisdom of Your Body and Mind to Face Stress, Pain, and Illness.* New York: Delta.

Levey, Joel. 1987. *The Fine Art of Relaxation, Concentration, and Meditation: Ancient Skills for Modern Life*. London: Wisdom.

Mason, John L. 1985. *Guide to Stress Reduction*. Berkeley, CA: Celestial Arts.

McKay, Matthew, Martha Davis, and Patrick Fanning. 1981. *Thoughts & Feelings: The Art of Cognitive Stress Intervention*. Oakland, CA: New Harbinger Publications.

Samuels, Mike, and Nancy Samuels. 1975. *Seeing with the Mind's Eye: The History, Techniques, and Uses of Visualization*. New York: Random House.

Tobias, Maxine, and Mary Stewart. 1985. *Stretch and Relax*. Tucson: Body Press.

Wells, Valerie. 1990. *The Joy of Visualization: 75 Creative Ways to Enhance Your Life*. San Francisco: Chronicle Books.

Coping with Anxiety

Bourne, Edmund J. 1995. *The Anxiety & Phobia Workbook*. 2nd ed. Oakland, CA: New Harbinger Publications.

DeRosis, Helen. 1979. *Women and Anxiety: A Step-By-Step Program to Overcome Your Anxieties*. New York: Delacorte.

Dowling, Colette. 1991. *You Mean I Don't Have to Feel This Way?: New Help for Depression, Anxiety, and Addiction*. New York: Scribner.

Fiore, Neil A., and Susan C. Pescar. 1987. *Conquering Test Anxiety*. New York: Warner.

Helmstetter, Shad. 1987. *The Self-Talk Solution*. New York: Pocket Books.

Kahn, Michael, and Allen Sandler. 1966. *A Manual for Self-Desensitization Therapy*. Yale University. Unpublished typescript.

Kent, Fraser. 1977. *Nothing to Fear: Coping with Phobias*. Garden City, NY: Doubleday.

Koestenbaum, Peter. 1974. *Managing Anxiety: The Power of Knowing Who You Are*. Englewood Cliffs, NJ: Prentice-Hall.

Lark, Susan M. 1993. *Anxiety and Stress: A Self-Help Program*. Los Altos, CA: Westchester Publishing.

Looper, Stan H., and Cynthia M. Scott. 1993. *When Anxiety Attacks: What the Health Care Community Doesn't Know about Anxiety*. New York: Swan.

Maloney, Michael, and Rachael Kranz. 1991. *Straight Talk about Anxiety and Depression*. New York: Dell.

Marks, Isaac M. 1978. *Living with Fear: Understanding and Coping with Anxiety.* New York: McGraw-Hill.

McCullough, Christopher J. 1991. *Always at Ease: Overcoming Shyness and Anxiety in Any Situation.* New York: Berkley Books.

McCullough, Christopher J., and Robert W. Mann. 1985. *Managing Your Anxiety: Regaining Control When You Feel Stressed, Helpless, and Alone.* Los Angeles: J.P. Tarcher.

Nideffer, Robert M., and Roger C. Sharpe. 1978. *How to Put Anxiety Behind You.* New York: Stein and Day.

Ottens, Allen J. 1984. *Coping with Academic Anxiety.* New York: Rosen Publishing Group.

Ross, Jerilyn. 1994. *Triumph over Fear.* New York: Bantam.

Seagrave, Ann, and Faison Covington. 1987. *Free from Fears: New Help for Anxiety, Panic, and Agoraphobia.* New York: Poseidon.

Smith, Manuel J. 1977. *Kicking the Fear Habit.* New York: Dial.

Wolpe, Joseph, with David Wolpe. 1988. *Life without Fear.* Oakland, CA: New Harbinger Publications.

Zuercher-White, Elke. 1995. *An End to Panic.* Oakland, CA: New Harbinger Publications.

Time Management and Study Skills

Alderson, Daniel. 1994. *SAT: See You at the Top.* Berkeley, CA: Celestial Arts.

Burka, J. B., and L. M. Yuen. 1983. *Procrastination: Why You Do It, and What to Do about It.* Reading, MA: Addison-Wesley.

Edelstein, Scott. 1991. *The Truth about College: How to Survive and Succeed as a Student in the Nineties.* Secaucus, NJ: Carol Publishing Group.

Ellis, David B. 1991. *Becoming a Master Student: Tools, Techniques, Hints, Ideas, Illustrations, Instructions, Examples, Methods, Procedures, Processes, Skills, Resources, and Suggestions for Success.* Rapid City, SD: College Survival.

Epstein, S. 1993. *You're Smarter Than You Think.* New York: Simon & Schuster.

Ferrari, J., J. Johnson, and W. McGown. 1995. *Procrastination and Task Avoidance: Theory, Research, and Treatment.* New York: Plenum.

Fiore, Neil. 1989. *The Now Habit: a Strategic Program for Overcoming Procrastination and Enjoying Guilt-free Play.* Los Angeles: Jeremy P. Tarcher.

Fry, Ronald W. 1994. *How to Study.* Hawthorne, NJ: Career Press.

Jansen, Eric. 1989. *Student Success Secrets.* New York: Barron's Educational Series.

Kornhauser, Arthur W. 1993. *How to Study: Suggestions for High-School and College Students.* Chicago: University of Chicago Press.

Lakein, Alan. 1973. *How to Get Control of Your Time and Your Life.* New York: Signet.

Nieves, Luis. 1984. *Coping in College: Successful Strategies.* Princeton: Educational Testing Service.

Pauk, Walter. 1989. *How to Study for College.* Boston: Houghton Mifflin.

Roberts, M. Susan. 1995. *Living without Procrastination.* Oakland, CA: New Harbinger Publications.

Scharf, D., and P. Hait. 1985. *Studying Smart.* New York: Harper and Row.

Scott, D. 1981. *How to Put More Time in Your Life.* New York: New American Library.

Siebert, Al. 1992. *Time for College: The Adult Student's Guide to Survival and Success.* Portland: Practical Psychology Press.

Stautberg, S. S., and M. L. Worthing. 1992. *Balancing Acts! Juggling Love, Work, Family, and Recreation.* New York: Master Media.

Winston, S. 1978. *Getting Organized.* New York: Warner Books.

Test-Taking Anxiety Research

Hall, R. A., and J. E. Hinkle. 1972. "Vicarious desensitization of test anxiety." *Behaviour Research and Therapy* 10:407–410.

Harris, G., and S. B. Johnson. 1980. "Comparison of individual covert modeling, self-control desensitization, and study skills training for alleviating test anxiety." *Journal of Consulting and Clinical Psychology* 48:186–194.

Harris, G., and S. B. Johnson. 1983. "Coping imagery and relaxation instructions in covert modeling treatment for test anxiety." *Behavior Therapy* 14:144–157.

Hill, K. T., and A. Wigfield. 1984. "Test anxiety: a major educational problem and what can be done about it." *The Elementary School Journal* 85(6):105–126.

Meichenbaum, D. 1972. "Cognitive modification of test-anxious college students." *Journal of Consulting and Clinical Psychology* 39:370–380.

Paulman, R. C., and K. J. Kennelly. 1984. "Test anxiety and ineffective test taking: different names same construct?" *Journal of Educational Psychology* 76(2):279–288.

Sapp, Marty. 1993. *Test Anxiety: Applied Research, Assessment, and Treatment Interventions.* Lanham, MA: University Press of America.

Sarason, I. G. 1973. "Test anxiety and cognitive modeling." *Journal of Personality and Social Psychology* 28:58–61.

Speilberger, C. D. 1980. *Test Anxiety Inventory.* Palo Alto, CA: Consulting Psychologist Press.

Suinn, R. M. 1970. "Short-term desensitization therapy." *Behaviour Research and Therapy* 8:383–384.

Wilson, N. H., and J. C. Rotter. 1986. "Anxiety management training and study skills counseling for students on self-esteem and test anxiety and performance. *The School Counselor* 34(1):18–31.

Wine, J. D. 1971. "Test anxiety and direction of attention." *Psychological Bulletin* 76:92–104.

Audiotapes

Budzynski, Thomas. 1981. "Relaxation Training Program." Three-tape set. New York: Guilford Publications. (800) 365-7006.

_____. 1985. "Stress Control." Trevose, PA: Futurehealth, Inc. (215) 364-4445.

Epstein-Shepherd, B. 1993. "Creating More Time in Your Life." Boulder, CO: Career Track Publications.

Miller, Emmett. 1980. "Letting Go of Stress." Menlo Park, CA: Source Cassettes. (415) 328-7171.

A number of audiotapes are available from New Harbinger Publications. Titles include "Hypnosis for Improved Learning," "Thought Stopping," "Systematic Desensitization and Visualizing Goals," and "Progressive Relaxation and Breathing." To order, call (800) 748-6273 or visit the Web site at www.newharbinger.com.